THORSONS GREEN COOKBOOK

About the author

Having graduated with a degree in home economics in 1979, Sarah Bounds joined the editorial staff of *Here's Health* magazine. She went on to become editor of that magazine, a post she chose to relinquish in October 1989 with the birth of her baby daughter Katy. She continues as a regular contributor to the magazine, writing on food and nutrition issues. Sarah, who lives in Woking, is also author of seven health related cookbooks, and she is deeply committed to a natural food philosophy.

THORSONS

GREEN
COOKBOOK

Food for a healthy future for you and the planet

SARAH BOUNDS

THORSONS

Thorsons Publishing Group

First published 1990

British Library Cataloguing in Publication Data

Bounds, Sarah
Thorsons green cookbook.
1. Health food dishes — Recipes
I. Title
641.5637

ISBN 0 7225 2423 4

*Published by Thorsons Publishers Limited, Wellingborough,
Northamptonshire NN8 2RQ, England*

Typeset by Harper Phototypesetters Limited, Northampton, England
Printed in Great Britain by Mackays, Chatham, Kent

3 5 7 9 10 8 6 4 2

For Katy

CONTENTS

INTRODUCTION

As the 1980s drew to a close a new consciousness stirred the world. The realization that the environment was under attack from man coloured the thinking of the public and of industry, commerce and government. Green issues such as global warming, the destruction of the rain forests, the hole in the ozone layer and the greenhouse effect entered the vocabulary and took centre stage on the political agenda. The fact that the way modern man has chosen to live is having potentially disastrous effects on the natural world began to hit home. The 1990s should see a change in our lifestyles if our children are to see the world survive.

Small changes are already happening. Unleaded petrol has flooded garage forecourts, street corners have sprouted bottle banks, washing powders are suddenly environmentally friendly and even birthday cards are being printed on recycled paper. Laudable though they are, these changes are only cosmetic changes. We still live in a polluting, throw-away society too eager to chuck out valuable resources, to use our cars and to sit back while industry, commerce and developers spoil our country-side. We take for granted our homes with their electrical gadgets; all we need to keep us in the comfort which we have so quickly come to expect. All the while we are consuming more electricity which is pro-duced in power stations which generate waste gases which, together with exhaust fumes from our cars, are contributing to global warming. This will lead to serious disruption in sea levels and climate throughout the world.

But there's more. If the world population continues to grow at the rate at which it is doing, there will come a time when there will not be enough land left to produce enough food to feed the world. We have come to expect a vast choice of food when we visit our local super-market with scarcely a thought for how it is produced. Food scares in the late 1980s — BSE, salmonella and listeria — have finally forced the issue in Britain. More and more people are cutting down on, or cutting out altogether, meat. Ironically, this could be our salvation. A mass reduction in the demand for meat and other animal foods which are more expensive to produce than plant foods such as cereals, nuts and pulses, could mean that in the long term agriculture will change and will change to a fairer system, producing enough food for us all to feel adequately fed.

These are the issues which are covered in The Green Cookbook. Complex issues but which briefly explained can help everyone to choose and to use foods which will not just benefit our own health but also that of the planet.

A THE THEORY

1 READY, STEADY, GO

Man eats to *live*, but in Western countries today it is easy to fall into the trap of living to *eat*. Food is plentiful, food is fun and food is fashionable. We respond to expensive food advertising by buying the latest flavour crisp, the latest shape in breakfast cereals and the latest development in ready-to-eat meals. At any one time, 40 per cent of Britons are overweight and struggling to lose weight, yet thousands of miles away, thousands, millions, even billions of people are struggling to find enough food to survive. We take an abundance of food very much for granted; those living in the developing countries are more likely to take *hunger* for granted. It seems grotesque that while we contemplate what — out of a fully stocked fridge — we'll eat for dinner tonight, there's little choice for millions living in countries where food supply has no hope of meeting the demands of its men, women and children. For them undernutrition is a way of life while we get fat from overnutrition. We are quite literally spoilt for choice.

MAKING CHOICES

Every day we have to choose what to eat — whether it's which filling to have in the lunch-time sandwich or which vegetables to chop up for the salad. The cook who's run out of ideas for original meals for the household plaintively cries, 'What shall we have for dinner tonight?' Eating is all about making choices and making an informed choice will give the best results. Too many choices are based on what we fancy, what is quick and what is easy. Choosing the right food, however, should mean choosing food that will meet the body's nutritional requirements. Man's immediate priority is to satisfy his hunger. Given that, in an affluent society, most people are in a position to do that, the priority should then be to satisfy the nutritional needs of our bodies. The *quality* of food then becomes more important than the *quantity*.

NUTRITION KNOW-HOW

The quality of any particular food can be assessed in many different ways. Looking through fresh vegetables on the market stall or supermarket display it's easy to pick out those items that look fresh, rejecting any battered, bruised or tired-looking specimens, but looks aren't all. Often organically grown produce looks inferior to the standardized chemical-grown foods; the former, however, will not contain any of the artificial agro-chemicals used to boost production and ensure uniformity of size and shape. There's another criteria of quality, too, and, essentially, this is the most important of all — it is also the most difficult to assess. The value of a food in terms of its value to the body is one that cannot be gauged accurately when we buy food — it's hardly practical to go shopping equipped with a mini-lab to measure the amount of vitamin C a particular orange contains, for example. In practice we have to call on our memory to tell us which foods to buy for a balanced diet. We know, or should know, that oranges are a better source of vitamin C than biscuits, that carrots, according to the old wive's tale, help to make you see in the dark (by virtue of the vitamin A the body metabolizes from them) and so on. Even the most basic nutritional knowledge can help form the basis of a moderately healthy shopping basket, but it does leave rather a large margin for error, given the influences from advertising, packaging and convenience. Choosing the right food for your body is rather like walking through a minefield, but making the right choices will equip the body to cope with all manner of attacks on its health. The basis of green eating is healthy eating and healthy eating has to start with a knowledge — however small — of nutrition.

FUEL CONSUMPTION

Just like a car or any other piece of machinery, we need fuel to be active. The body uses this fuel, converting it into energy in two basic different ways. First, in the fundamental process of living — the basal metabolism — which goes on night and day without our really being aware of it, maintaining breathing, brain function, heart beat, digestion, body temperature and more. An adult man needs a calorie every minute, every hour, every day just to keep the body 'ticking over', to keep alive. During a good eight-hour sleep at night, more than 400 calories are used up while the body and brain rest. The basal, or resting, metabolism is our basic energy need. During the course of a day we expend more energy as we move — the more strenuous that activity, the greater the energy consumption, and the greater our need for calories to satisfy that need. Sitting at a desk takes 1.4 calories a minute, walking slowly takes 3, while walking up and down stairs takes 9 calories every minute. So, a computer operator sitting at a VDU screen will burn up considerably fewer calories than will the young mother running around after her children all day, or the coal miner working down the pit.

Energy expenditure dictates our energy needs. Too much energy taken in as too many calories from food will be stored in the body. The surplus is stored first in the liver and then in the fat that gradually builds up until one day our clothes won't fit and the mirror reveals bulges where there used to be streamlined flesh and the scales reach a new high. That is what middle-age spread is all about — the result of years of eating just a little bit too much, just a little bit more than we burn off. Weighing more than the ideal weight for our height and frame means unsightly bulges, but being overweight in the extreme has more serious implications for our health, too. Coronary heart disease and late-onset diabetes are both more likely to occur when there is a serious weight problem, and if an overweight person needs surgery, the risks of complications are far higher. Losing extra weight will not only help you *look* good, it will help you *feel* good and will positively *do* you good, too.

FUEL RATING

The calorific value of food tells you how much energy will be produced in the body when it is consumed. Some foods simply supply calories and little else in the way of valuable nutrients. White sugar is the perfect example of this, supplying only empty calories — pure sweetness, pure calories and virtually nothing else. On a star rating system, this food is definitely a two-star. It is fine for getting us moving, but it carries no guarantee of any quality of performance in terms of the vital body processes which depend on nutrients for their correct function. Four-star foods, rather like four-star petrol, will give movement, energy *and* performance. The more nutrients a food contains in addition to its calorific value, the greater its value to the body. In a world where resources are in increasingly short supply, why bother with two-star food? Maximize resources by choosing four-star foods that will be of maximum benefit to the body, too.

FOUR-STAR FOODS

Four-star foods are foods that should form the basis of a healthy diet. Maximum nutrition from the minimum of bulk is an efficient way of eating. It is efficient, too, in making the best use of valuable land and agricultural resources; efficient in making our bodies work at an optimum level, boosting health and making us feel good. So what are the nutrients we need, beyond calories, to keep the body running smoothly?

● **Protein**: Protein is the basis of every cell in the body. Protein gives structure to bones, hair, nails and teeth. It forms the basis of muscles and organs, of hormones, enzymes and blood. Protein is vitally important to man, animal and plant. Proteins are extremely complex substances and there are many different types, just as there are many different sources of protein in the body. Each protein comprises of a slightly different composition of amino acids, the building blocks of protein. In all there are 20 different amino acids 8 of which are said to be essential amino acids.

In our bodies, amino acids are broken down and used in different ways. The body is able to 'make' the other 12 amino acids, so the 8 must be supplied to the body in the food we eat. The more of these essential amino acids a food contains, the better the quality of its protein content. Perhaps not surprisingly, animal foods contain better quality proteins in general than do plant foods, which tend to lack one or be short of several, depending on the family of plants they belong to. This forms the basis of protein combining, which it is vital that vegans and vegetarians understand as they eat no or little animal proteins respectively. And for those of us interested in eating a 'greener' diet, it is equally important to grasp this fundamental fact. Protein plays such a basic, vital role in our health that we all need to consume essential amino acids at every meal — young children, pregnant and breast-feeding mums even more so.

If meat, fish and poultry or dairy products aren't being eaten, it is important to mix different types of plant protein foods together to obtain a good balance of amino acids. So pulses (lentils, split peas, beans and so on) should be mixed with nuts or grains (rice, wheat, oats, rye, millet, for example) to form complete proteins. This is the golden rule of protein combining, however if animal foods are also eaten, it is sufficient to eat a pulse or a grain or nut with any one animal food to ensure complete protein is supplied. So, wheat-based breakfast cereal eaten with milk, or a cheese sandwich, or chilli con carne will make the proteins in the wheat, bread and red kidney beans complete.

The quantity of protein eaten in Western societies does not generally give any cause for concern. We tend to eat adequate amounts (not so the thousands of starving men, women and children in developing countries where protein is often in desperately short supply). The abundance of protein, as of food, for affluent societies contrasts poignantly with the shortage of both protein and food in poor nations and calls into question the whole ethics of modern food production (see Chapter 2).

● **Vitamins**: Vitamins are substances needed for health. They cannot be made in the body so they must be present in the food we eat. A shortage of any one vitamin will cause specific deficiency symptoms, some of them minor, others, if prolonged, resulting in quite severe diseases.

Vitamins are basically divided into two groups: the fat-soluble vitamins (A, D, E and L) and the water-soluble (B group and C).

The water-soluble vitamins are more fragile than the fat-soluble vitamins, being prone to destruction by heat during food processing and cooking and dissolved out from food when it is cooked in water (you lose all the valuable vitamins when you drain boiled vegetables). Once in the body, alcohol, tobacco and certain pharmaceutical drugs will destroy vitamins and interfere with their functioning.

Researchers are discovering that certain illnesses can be treated by taking large doses of vitamin supplements. Vitamin C, for example boosts immunity, vitamin E aids the heart and blood circulation and the B vitamins can help with mental disorders. One of the best sources of information I have found on this aspect of vitamins is *Nutritional Medicine* by Dr Stephen Davies and Dr Alan Stewart (Pan, 1987).

The role vitamins play and the best food sources of each are summarized in Table 1. The less we process a food, the better preserved its original vitamin level will be. B vitamins and vitamin E, for example, are lost when whole grain cereals are refined, while high temperatures used in processing fruit and vegetables (with the exception of freezing) will tend to destroy vitamins C and B. Storage, too, leads to a gradual decline in the level of vitamin C in fresh produce, so the fresher food can be eaten the better it will be for us — and with the minimum amount of delay and cooking in the kitchen too.

Table 1: The Major Vitamins and Their Value to Health

Vitamin	Action	Food sources
Vitamin A	Healthy skin, tissues and bone. Resistance to infection. Vision, especially in dim light. Growth in young children.	Cod-liver oil, liver, kidney, dairy produce, fish. Body converts carotene in green, yellow and orange fruit and vegetables to A: apricots, carrots, tomatoes, spinach and other green, leafy vegetables.
Vitamin B$_1$ (thiamin)	Energy release from food. Healthy nerves.	Brewer's yeast, wheatgerm, grains, nuts, pulses, yeast extract, meat vegetables.
Vitamin B$_2$ (riboflavin)	Energy release from food. Repair of body tissue.	Brewer's yeast, yeast extract, wheatgerm, liver, milk, eggs, green vegetables.
Vitamin B$_3$ (niacin)	Energy release from food and synthesis of protein and fat. Healthy gastro-intestinal tract, skin, nerves, cells.	Brewer's yeast, yeast extract, bran, nuts, grains, poultry, meat and milk.
Vitamin B$_6$	Protein metabolism and red blood cells.	Brewer's yeast, yeast extract, wheatgerm, eggs, whole grains, meat, fish, eggs, nuts, pulses, bananas, green and root vegetables.

Vitamin	Action	Food sources
Vitamin B$_{12}$	For red blood cells and nerve cells.	Liver, fish, eggs, meat, dairy produce. Not found in plants — only vegetable source is spirulina.
Vitamin C	Resistance to infection, healthy skin, wound healing, formation of connective tissues.	Fruits and vegetables, especially blackcurrants, citrus fruits, sprouted beans, guavas, kale, green peppers, Brussels sprouts.
Vitamin D	Healthy formation of bones and teeth, blood and tissue.	Fish-liver oils, oily fish, butter and margarine, directly from the action of sun on the skin.
Vitamin E	As antioxidant, protects cells from destructive agents, strengthens blood circulation.	Wheatgerm oil, other vegetable oils, nuts, shellfish, egg yolk, grains, green vegetables.
Biotin	Metabolism of fat, protein and carbohydrates.	Brewer's yeast, eggs, liver, kidney, fish, fruit and vegetables, dairy produce.
Folic acid	In red blood cells, protein synthesis and in building babies' resistance to infection.	Brewer's yeast, liver, kidney, green leafy vegetables, pulses, nuts, grains, bananas, oranges, wheatgerm.
Pantothenic acid	Energy release from food, production of antibodies, growth.	Brewer's yeast, nuts, pulses, liver, grains and eggs.

● **Minerals**: Minerals, like vitamins, are needed by the body in relatively small quantities, but there are huge differences in the amounts of each mineral required. Calcium, for example, is required in large quantities — babies up to a year old need a huge 600mg a day. Selenium, on the other hand, is required by babies in tiny amounts from 10-40mg daily (1,000mcg = 1mg).

Minerals cannot be destroyed by heat so are more stable than the water-soluble vitamins, but they can be removed from food by processing and refining and simply combine with other substances in food so that the body cannot absorb them. When there is insufficient quantity of a mineral in the body then deficiency symptoms develop that if prolonged, can become severe.

The mineral content of food varies widely because plants can only absorb minerals if they are present in the soil, so it follows that poor soil will produce poor quality plants short of vital minerals. Whole regions can be either richly or poorly supplied by minerals where there are above- or below-average quantities of that mineral naturally present in the soil. Organic farming, which involves taking care to replenish the soil's natural goodness, is likely to produce mineral-rich plants; modern farming, on the other hand, relies on chemicals to do the job of building soil quality. The major minerals are summarized in Table 2.

Table 2: The Major Minerals and Their Value to Health

Mineral	Action	Food sources
Calcium	Formation of bones and teeth, control of muscles and nerves and blood clotting.	Milk, cheese, wholemeal bread and flour, green vegetables and fish eaten with bones.
Chromium	For metabolizing glucose in the body.	Brewer's yeast, liver, cheese, wheatgerm, fish, wholegrain cereals.
Iodine	For formation of thyroxine hormone, which controls metabolic rate.	Seaweeds, seafoods and produce grown in soils enriched with seaweed.
Iron	Formation of red blood cells.	Liver, kidney and red meat, wholemeal bread and flour, egg yolk, green vegetables, dried apricots.
Magnesium	Essential for all body cells and for release of energy from food.	Found in most foods, fruit and vegetables in particular.
Manganese	For growth and reproduction, defence against infection, and synthesizing glucose, fat and carbohydrate.	Wholegrain cereals, avocados, pulses, many fruits and green vegeetables.

Mineral	Action	Food sources
Phosphorus	Involved with calcium in bones and teeth, helps metabolism of protein, fat and B vitamins and release of energy.	Widely found in food, especially dairy produce, poultry, wholemeal bread and fish.
Selenium	As antioxidant in protecting cells from free-radical attack.	Wholegrain cereals, fish, liver, fruits and vegetables.
Zinc	For growth and development, especially of sex organs. For healthy skin and for metabolizing vitamin A.	Fish, especially oysters, liver, eggs, and wholegrain cereals.

● **Fats**: Protein, vitamins and minerals all play a positive role in maintaining health, but fat, while essential in small amounts, is more likely to exert a negative, detrimental effect on health. Fat is a highly concentrated source of calories and the typical Western diet simply contains too much fat, particularly saturated fat from red meat and dairy produce. Generally vegetarians (unless they depend too heavily on cheese and eggs rather than plant foods) and vegans have a lower intake of fat than carnivores and, in the long term, that is likely to mean fewer weight problems and possibly healthier hearts, too.

We do need to have some fat in our diet and the essential fatty acids, as their name suggests, must be present. These are linoleic acid and linolenic acid, and both are found in vegetable fats, with safflower and sunflower oils being especially good sources. So we can safely reduce or cut out the hard animal fats from our diet and cut down on fatty foods, such as fried foods, cream cakes and puddings. In addition to linoleic and linolenic acids, both of which are polyunsaturated fatty acids, there are two other fatty acids of this type that are beginning to attract interest. These are DHA and EPA, two fatty acids that are found in oily fish, such as herring and mackerel, and, while not essential for health, are believed to play a part in protecting against heart disease.

● **Carbohydrates**: Carbohydrates are energy-giving foods and, like fats, some are better for the body than others. Complex carbohydrates, found in unrefined cereals like brown rice and wholemeal flour, along with dietary fibre, are better at fuelling the body's activities because they take longer to digest. Instead of the sudden surge of sugar into the bloodstream that occurs when sugar or glucose-rich foods and drinks are consumed, there is a more controlled release of energy. This puts less strain on the pancreas, which regulates blood-sugar levels, and helps us to feel full for longer, so avoiding the temptation to snack between meals. Fibre in itself plays a vital role in preventing constipation and other problems relating to the passage of food through the body and is found in wholegrain cereals, pulses (including both dried beans and fresh peas and so on) as well as in fresh fruits and other vegetables.

THE FIGHTERS

Staying healthy reflects our ability to fight infection, which in turn relies on our in-built system of defences to cope with bacteria, viruses and toxic substances to which the body is exposed. In today's modern world we are subjected to a whole host of toxic chemicals in the environment: our air is polluted with lead, carbon monoxide and nitrogen oxide, our water with nitrates, chlorine and aluminium, our food with agro-chemicals and additives and our homes with cleaning fluids, detergents and possibly leaky gas appliances.

In the face of such an onslaught, great strain is being put on the body's defence capabilities. At the core of those defences are the antioxidants that react to the so-called free radicals that are produced by stresses such as these. Antioxidants include certain vitamins, minerals and enzymes that work in unison to protect the body from free-radical damage. The antioxidant nutrients are:

● vitamin A — as beta carotene
● vitamin C
● vitamin E
● selenium — as selenium containing amino acids
● manganese, zinc and copper — as the enzyme superoxide dismutase

All these essential nutrients are involved with fighting toxins in the body. They boost enzyme activity and also help to remove the offending substances from the body.

Fibre, especially the form of fibre that is found in wheat bran and present in wholewheat flour, bread and pasta, also contributes to the body's defence system. Because fibre speeds up the passage of waste material through the body, it takes with it toxins before they have the chance to act and cause harm.

TAKE ACTION

RED: AVOID
● Sugar and sugar-rich foods: cakes, biscuits and sweet pastries, confectionery.

- Fried foods: chips, foods that have been cooked in large amounts of fat.
- Fatty foods: foods where the fat is clearly visible, such as fatty cuts of meat, cream cakes.
- Foods containing artificial additives: preservatives, colourings, flavourings and so on.

AMBER: RESTRICT
- Dairy produce: skimmed rather than full-fat milk, free-range or perechery eggs rather than factory-farmed, farmhouse cheeses rather than factory cheese.
- Red meat and offal: beef, pork and lamb, liver and kidney.
- Poultry: choose free-range rather than factory-farmed.
- Fish: choose white and oily fish, shellfish.

GREEN: BE GENEROUS
- Grains: wheat — wholewheat flour, bread, pasta, cracked wheat; brown rice; oats — oatflakes, rolled oats and oatmeal; millet; buckwheat; rye flour; maize (corn) — cornmeal (not cornflour).
- Pulses: beans — all dried beans, such as butter, aduki, haricot, soya, flageolet; beansprouts; lentils; split peas.
- Nuts: almonds, cashews, walnuts, brazils, pine kernels, chestnuts, peanuts and peanut butter.
- Seeds: sesame, sunflower, pumpkin.
- All vegetables, especially root vegetables and leafy green vegetables.
- All fruits, especially orange/yellow-coloured fruits.

2 FOOD FROM THE LAND

In the past few years, modern farming methods have been brought to the attention of the British public through two major incidents. First came the chicken and the egg scandal — the problem of the widespread contamination of poultry with the food poisoning bacteria salmonella. Then came the bovine spongiform encephalopathy, or BSE epidemic that threatens the production of beef in Britain and poses questions over the production of poultry and pork, too, as feedstuffs made from animal by-products continue to be used in these farm animal's diets. The British public have finally woken up to the way that food is produced today and the picture is hardly appetizing. It is as far removed from our cosy images of cattle and sheep grazing contentedly in green pastures as it's possible to imagine. With a few exceptions farm animals are treated as little more than machines — looked on as units to be fed and watered before being slaughtered for profit, and very hungry machines at that.

Eight per cent of all farmland in Britain is used to grow crops for man to eat, while the rest is used to produce animal feed. Ten pounds (4.5kg) of plant material is needed to produce one pound (455g) of animal flesh for man.

The wastefulness and other negative factors of this system must be considered in context. With a global population explosion in Asia, Africa and other developing countries, can we really afford the luxury of eating meat when millions of these people cannot find food?

The statistics make grim reading. 10 acres of land will grow enough to support: 61 people on a diet of soya beans; 24 people on a diet of wheat; 10 people on a diet of maize; 2 people on a diet of cattle meat. (Figures from The Vegetarian Society.) It is clear from this that raising animals for meat is not an efficient means of using land to produce food. Much more economical would be to feed man the plants directly rather than indirectly through livestock.

David Icke, spokesman for the Green Party says in his book *It Doesn't Have to be Like This* (Green Print, 1990) that Britain could be more than self-sufficient if we all gave up eating meat and became vegetarians: 'This country could feed a population of 250 million on an all-vegetarian diet without any food imports. We have 57 million'. And not only do we import food from traditionally rich agricultural lands such as America and Australia and other EEC nations, we also import food from developing countries where hunger and malnutrition are rife. Again David Icke states that in 1984, at the height of international concern over the Ethiopian famine, Britain imported £1.5

million worth of food to feed our livestock. The people of developing countries like Ethiopia are often encouraged to grow cash crops like coffee, sugar and tea rather than food crops that would feed themselves and their families.

The food problem is not global, it is local. Food is incorrectly and unfairly distributed giving affluent countries a surplus while developing nations go short. Adding that extra link in the food chain in the form of animal livestock just makes the problem worse.

It is unrealistic to expect billions of people living in affluent countries to suddenly change the habits of a lifetime and give up meat — or is it? Already in Britain the trend towards vegetarianism is happening. Whether it's for moral, ethical or health reasons, there is a very definite move away from red meat in particular among the British people. Recent market research carried out for Realeat, a pioneering vegetarian food manufacturer, shows that one in five young people aged between 16 and 24 are now vegetarian, that 40 per cent of the population are cutting down on their consumption of red meat and predicts that in 20 years' time at least half the British people will be eating a vegetable-based diet. The implication for the food industry is enormous. The implication if this trend is to be repeated in other European and Western style nations could be staggering in its effects on the global food supply.

As the move away from meat gathers momentum so does the demand for chemical-free food. While salmonella and BSE grabbed the biggest headlines, there have also been scares about pesticides in food, in particular that of Alar. The potential risks from exposure to pesticide-sprayed foods has highlighted the safety of these and other common agro-chemicals in a way that many campaigners have been hoping for years.

Organic food has enjoyed much publicity as the benefits of eating food free from agro-chemicals has been widely discussed and agreed upon. However, while it is easy to give up meat simply by not buying it, it is not so easy to reject one form of food if the other, safer form is not always available. The current situation for organic food is that poor availability and often high prices limit its potential uptake among the general public. Consumer demand for organic food is on the increase, however, and researchers suggest that we will have to double the production of organic food in the next few years if consumer demand is to be satisfied. Now the pressure is on the Government to help make organic food more widely available by giving the necessary support to farmers to make what is a long-term and costly conversion away from modern intensive farming to a more natural, organic system of food production.

The appeal of organic food is the absence of pesticides, herbicides, fungicides and all manner of farm chemicals used by today's intensive methods of producing food. Traces of these potent substances can remain in the food and, so widespead is the use of chemicals in the growing and storage after harvest of all manner of foods that, as we sit down to a meal we are likely to be swallowing unwittingly a chemical cocktail and just what the effect in the long term such a cocktail might have on the body is not known. Organic food, on the other hand, contains none of these new synthetic substances. Organic food is produced on farms where natural 'fertilizers', like seaweed and manure, and traditional methods of agriculture, such as crop rotation, are used to produce healthy food in a way that is more beneficial to man and to the land. This last 'by-product' is the crucial added advantage of organic food — it benefits both our health *and* that of the environment. Organic farmers do not use the high levels of nitrates that pollute waterways, they don't tear down hedges to make way for vast priarie-like fields that destroy the natural habitat for wildlife and they don't use chemicals that can harm birds and animals in the wild and harm us at the table.

Organic farming has much to offer and the potential for growth is enormous. There are about 1,000 organic farms in the UK — out of a total of 244,000 farms. Critics say that chemicals are vital to give farmers the yields they need from the land, but that is a myth. Today's British farmers are being encouraged to take farm land out of production to help cut down on the production of *surpluses*. Organics do produce a smaller yield per acre — about 20 per cent less — but they do that without any environmental pollution, destruction of wildlife or risk to health. Isn't it time it was taken seriously by the government and incentives were given to encourage farmers not to leave farmland idle or convert it into golf courses or leisure facilities, but instead convert it to *real* farmland that will produce *real* food? The Prince of Wales is known for his support of the organic movement and has been experimenting with organics on Duchy of Cornwall farms. In a message of support to the 1989 national conference on Organic Food Production Prince Charles said, 'It is now that farmers and policy makers must be shown that organic farming is a viable approach to agriculture and that it is one means of dealing with the problems caused by modern intensive farming methods'.

WHERE TO BUY ORGANIC FOOD

SHOPS
Organic food can be found in specialist wholefood and healthfood shops and in an increasing number of supermarkets — Safeway, Sainsbury, Tesco and some branches of Marks & Spencer and Waitrose.

Sometimes only the word 'organic' on the packaging distinguishes a food from its conventionally grown counterpart. This gives little guarantee to the consumer that the produce is genuinely organic. However there are several symbols that you might see on packaging or labelling.

First, and most important, is the Soil Association symbol that is used by farmers, processors and growers who conform to the Soil Association's strict

organic standards.

Another logo from Organic Farmers and Growers is sometimes used and in the future the symbol of the Government's new set of organic standards — UKROFS — will also appear. In addition, food may be labelled 'conservation grade'. This term covers a type of half-way style of agriculture, that is half-way between chemicals and organics — and is often used when a farmer is in the process of converting from conventional farming methods to organics. It takes up to seven years for a farm to become fully organic and the process is highly complex and this is why some guarantee of authenticity is essential for the consumer.

FRESH FROM THE FARM GATE

Many of the Soil Association's symbol holders have farm shops or offer consumers the chance to buy organic produce on a less formal basis. The list in the Appendix, page 141, details the Soil Association farms throughout Britain where you can buy produce fresh from the farm. It's best to phone first to check that they will sell their foods in small amounts.

3 ENERGY IN THE HOME

Global warming, acid rain, the greenhouse effect and rainforest destruction are phrases that have all become part of our vocabulary. In the past two years environmental issues have taken centre stage in the political debate as governments the world over have been forced to confront the problems facing the environment. Campaigners have set the alarm bells ringing; now at last the pressure they have been exerting is paying off as world leaders are being forced to take action in an effort to try to halt some of the most serious effects our pollution is having on the planet.

ENERGY EQUATION

How we obtain energy to fuel our cars, heat our homes and power industry and commerce is at the core of the debate. The production of large amounts of carbon dioxide in the generation of electricity and from fuel exhausts is directly linked to the phenomenon of global warming. Governments have been forced to agree to cut emissions of carbon dioxide in the face of research which states that, unless drastic steps are taken, the global temperature will rise by 2°C by the year 2030. This would have severe implications, not just on climate but also on the nature of the land as sea levels will rise and flood low-lying areas of continents.

As well as energy production, energy conservation needs to feature more prominently. The equation is simple: the less energy we consume, the less energy will need to be produced and the less severe the threat. Friends of the Earth state that we already have the technology to cut energy demand by 70 per cent and argue that a greater emphasis needs to be put on the renewable sources of energy, such as solar, tidal and wind power. Our reliance on fossil fuels (oil, coal, gas) means that 75 per cent of carbon dioxide in the atmosphere comes from them. The generation of electricity accounts for more than a third of that and the UK government favours reducing that figure in preference to the 18 per cent that comes directly from car exhausts.

HOME SAVINGS

Of all the electricity produced in Britain, over a third is used in the home to keep us warm, feed and clean us. This is where the power goes:

- heating, 23 per cent
- water heating, 18 per cent
- cooking, 10 per cent
- lighting, 8 per cent
- all other appliances, 41 per cent

HEATING

The average central heating system, in an average three-bedroomed home, uses 14,000 kw hours a year, but much of the heat produced is lost. In a poorly insulated home, the heat loss can be as much as 75 per cent. According to the Centre for Alternative Technology, this loss is made up like this:

- 25 per cent escapes through the walls
- 20 per cent escapes through the roof
- 10 per cent escapes through the windows
- 10 per cent escapes through the floor
- 10 per cent escapes through draughts.

It's easy to see how very simple measures — such as loft insulation, heavy carpets, lined curtains and draughtproofing — can help to reduce such a waste. The Government-run Energy Efficiency Office at the Department of Energy focusses on the savings that can be made in fuel consumption and thus on fuel bills by the following measures, and in brackets tells how soon the initial outlay can be recouped:

- hot-water cylinder insulation (one year)
- pipe insultation (one year)
- radiator foil (two years)
- draughtproofing (two years)
- loft insulation (two years)
- cavity wall insulation (three to five years)
- boiler replacement (three to five years)
- heating system programmer (three to five years)
- thermostatic valves (three to five years).

Turning down the thermostat on the central heating by just 1°C can save as much as 10 per cent of your energy consumption, say Friends of the Earth. Another factor affecting your energy consumption in heating your home is the type of boiler used. The most energy efficient boiler for central heating is the gas condenser type. These are more expensive initially than conventional boilers, but are up to 20 per cent more efficient than other modern boilers and 30 per cent better than old boilers. So, if you are considering replacing your boiler, it is worth investing in a gas condenser type as the initial outlay will be recouped in two to three years. Other energy saving tips worth considering for heating and hot water are:

● making full use of time control mechanisms to avoid heating the house when it's empty, using the timer to turn on the heating just before it's needed and turn it off when the house is empty
● not blocking the circulation of hot air from radiators with curtains or furniture
● fixing radiator foil behind radiators sited on outside walls to reflect heat back into the room
● installing foam or metal draught excluder strips around external doors and windows
● insulating the loft space, for as much as one fifth of your energy bills can be saved by this simple measure (some householders are eligible for government grants)
● considering cavity wall insulation and double glazing (the former gives a better return on investment)
● considering thermostatic room and radiator controls
● lagging the hot water tank and hot and cold water pipes in the loft
● always turning off taps and fixing any that drip
● taking a shower in preference to a bath — a shower uses half the amount of hot water.

COOKING

Saving energy in the preparation of food depends on the appliances used. If yours is an automated kitchen with an electric can opener, a food processor to perform a whole battery of tasks, from chopping to shredding, then, even before food is cooked with heat from a hob, grill or oven, energy is obviously being consumed. Many, but not all, kitchen gadgets save time and the user's energy in performing menial tasks; others simply guzzle energy and don't give much in the way of saving other resources. Energy savings can be made in most kitchens, however, regardless of other factors:

THE COOKER

Gas cookers are more expensive to buy than electric cookers with the same features, but gas cookers are cheaper to run. Whatever the fuel, the following energy saving tips can apply:

● **the hob:** choose saucepans that fit the hotplate well so that energy is not wasted in heating areas not in contact with the base of the pan, and if using gas, adjust the flame height so that it just covers the saucepan base; cook produce in the minimum of water for better retention of water-soluble vitamins B and C and to save energy by not heating up an unnecessary volume of water; turn down the heat once the contents of the pan have come to the boil (unless recipe states otherwise, e.g. pasta that needs to boil constantly) — electric hot plates retain the heat well so can be turned down low and the pan will still receive adequate heat — the material of the pan also affects heat retention with enamelled cast iron being especially good at retaining heat once hot and therefore in conserving energy (the different types of electric hotplate differ in their speed in heating up with sealed hotplates taking the longest to heat up and cool down and radiant rings heating up and cooling down quickly, ceramic hobs heating up slowly and cooling down fairly slowly, and the newest style halogen hobs heating up quickly, but cooling down slowly; always cook with the lid, unless the recipe states otherwise (pasta will boil over with a lid on)

● **the grill:** toasters consume less energy than grills for cooking toast, but some grills in electric ovens have a dual capacity enabling a small area — usually half — to be heated up and this saves energy if only a small grilling surface is required.

● **the oven**: if buying a new oven, check that there is a good level of insulation surrounding the oven to cut down heat loss — some appliance manufacturers are improving this aspect in a bid to save energy consumption so it is worth comparing models; a glass inner door to the oven or a glass panel in the outer door combined with an oven light can reduce the number of times you need to open the oven door to check how food is cooking — the more the door is opened when the oven is on, the greater the heat loss; fan-assisted ovens are more expensive features initially, but they are energy saving as they heat up more quickly than conventional ovens, reducing the time taken to cook foods and improving also the heat distribution within the oven itself, as food cooks at the same rate in the various shelf positions, whereas in conventional cookers the hottest place is at the top so food can be cooked at a lower oven temperature and in less time too; for small amounts of food, a smaller oven in a double oven cooker can be used to cut down the amount of energy required to heat up a large oven space and always make full use of oven space anyway by batch-baking (see Chapter 9) or by cooking accompaniments or a pudding, say at the same time as the main course, and some single-pot recipes for casseroles could well be cooked slowly on the hob rather than in the oven.

THE PRESSURE COOKER

The pressure cooker is by no means a recent addition to the kitchen and in many ways its role in saving time has been overlooked by the microwave's surge in popularity in the 1980s. In the energy conscious 90s, however, surely it's time to reassess the role of the pressure cooker in preparing food.

The pressure cooker saves energy by reducing cooking times by two thirds, using only the energy needed to heat a ring on the hob to do so. In fact, once the cooker has reached the desired level of pressure, the heat can be turned down to a very low setting to maintain that pressure.

Many foods can be pressure-cooked successfully — plain vegetables and fruits, pulses, rice and pasta, boiling joints of bacon and ham, stocks and recipe dishes such as soups, stews, casseroles, sauces and some puddings (especially the unhealthy, steamed variety and Christmas pud!) Many of the recipes for soups and casseroles in this book could be prepared in the pressure cooker, but in converting recipes for the pressure cooker, it is best to refer to the manufacturer's handbook for general instructions on types of dishes for your specific model of pressure cooker.

One popular use of the pressure cooker, is in the preparation of pre-cooked pulses for recipes. Cooking pre-soaked beans, peas and lentils in the pressure cooker is not only far quicker, it is much easier than having to watch that pans of boiling pulses don't burn dry or overcook. Here's a general guide for some of the most popular types of pulses, all requiring pre-soaking before cooking at 15 lb pressure.

Pulse	Soaking time	Pressure cooking time
Lentils	1 hour	5 minutes
Aduki	8-10 hours	10 minutes
Black eye	8-10 hours	10 minutes
Borlotti	8-10 hours	10 minutes
Butter	8-10 hours	10 minutes
Chick peas	8-10 hours	10 minutes
Flageolet	8-10 hours	10 minutes
Haricot	8-10 hours	10 minutes
Kidney beans	8-10 hours	15 minutes
Soya beans	12 hours	25 minutes

THE MICROWAVE OVEN

The microwave oven steadily grew in popularity throughout the 1970s and 1980s until late in 1989 when research showed that extra care was needed in the reheating of foods, particularly commercially prepared cook-chill foods where some contamination with food poisoning organisms was most likely to occur and which needed a high temperature during reheating to kill any such bacteria. This sounded a warning note — one of the few — against an appliance that a vast number of people now own and value for its time-saving convenience and unique ability to thaw food from frozen.

Microwaves undoubtedly save energy, taking less time to cook foods than the conventional methods, but there are cases when more energy is consumed, for example when food is thawed in the microwave instead of being left to thaw at room temperature and in reheating food that would otherwise be served cold. Because of the way in which microwaves function, that is, food is heated by the friction produced by the microwaves, cooking time increases proportionately with the amount of food in the oven. Cooking time will also be influenced by the type of container being used, the initial temperature of the food and its structure. On the other hand, energy is saved in comparison to conventional cooking as little heat is lost to the air because the oven doesn't become hot itself, only the food heats up.

Microwaves do perform differently — lack of browning, lack of flavour development — but to some extent these differences are overcome in combination ovens where hot air is used in conjunction with microwaves to cook the food. Nutritionally, the heat-sensitive vitamins B and C are thought to be better preserved, particularly in fruit and vegetables as cooking times are short and little fluid is required during cooking. There are those who feel that the action of the microwaves so alters food that its vital life force is destroyed and its value to the body lost. In many ways microwave ovens are viewed subjectively and are very much influenced by individual attitudes to them. Objectively, however, there is little disputing the fact that they usually do save cooking times and hence save energy consumption, but this has to be set against the relatively high purchase price.

THE SLOW COOKER

Whereas microwaves and pressure cookers score by the speed with which they cook, the slow cooker has the potential to save energy by virtue of its low wattage, consuming a small amount of energy but over a long period of time. It can save fuel, but how great these savings are depends on the individual fuel consumption of each model (the bigger the slow cooker the higher the fuel consumption) and on the setting at which food is cooked.

Food cooks differently in the slow cooker because the temperatures reached are low. Vegetables take longer to soften than does meat and so they must be cut extremely finely to cook through and dried beans must not only be pre-soaked, they must also be boiled for 10 minutes before being put into the slow cooker. The nutritional content of food is also likely to be lowered by the long exposure to heat. These points, plus the fact that they are only suited to casseroles, soups and stews in the main, does limit their value.

LIGHTING

Turning off lights in rooms or hallways that are not being used is an obvious and immediate energy saving tip, but further savings are possible with the advent of energy efficient lighting. These new style fluorescent tubes use 75 per cent less electricity than conventional filament bulbs but produce the same amount of light and can last up to eight times as long.

APPLIANCES

A look around an average home reveals a host of electrical appliances that we use to carry out many diverse functions: television, hi-fi, video, dishwasher, washing machine, tumble drier, fridge, freezer, food processor, microwave, vacuum cleaner, iron, kettle, toaster, hair dryer, razor — the list is long and the energy consumption large. The approximate running costs for these appliances given in Table 3 show just how much gadgets increase fuel bills and add to your home's energy consumption. If you multiply this across the country, the figures are incredible. Did you know that the TV sets tuned to one episode of *Neighbours* will consume £60,000 worth of electricity and therefore release 1,000 tonnes of carbon dioxide, 12 tonnes of sulphur dioxide and 3.5 tonnes of nitrous oxide in to the atmosphere.

Table 3: Quarterly Cost of Appliances

Item	Used for	Approximate cost per quarter
2kw fan heater/bar fire	3 hours a day	£35
Electric oven	meals for four	£12.70-£16.20
Dishwasher	1 load a day	£11.50
Tumble drier	4 loads	£10.40
Washing machine	5 washes	£4.60-£9.20
Fridge-freezer	6.5/3 cu ft (0.18/0.08 cu m)	£10.50
Upright freezer	6 cu ft (0.17 cu m)	£8
Fridge	3.5 cu ft (0.09 cu m)	£3.50
Kettle	8 pts (4.5 l) a day	£3.50
Electric shower	1 a day	£3.50
Combination microwave	15 min daily on high	£3.50
Microwave oven	10 min daily on high	75p
Colour TV	3 hours a day	£2.90
100W light bulb	5 hours a day	£2.90
Toaster	8 slices daily	70p

(These figures are amended from *Which* magazine, September 1987. Running costs vary with wattage on individual appliances.)

Manufacturers of domestic appliances are beginning to respond to environmental concerns by lowering the energy consumption of many appliances. The 'green machines' that are beginning to appear in shops have, at their simplest, a lower wattage than conventional appliances and may also possess other so-called environmentally friendly features (see page 35). If you are buying electrical appliances, it's worth comparing the wattage on different brands. Hopefully new labelling initiatives will make it easier to do this to identify where energy savings can be made.

4 THE GREEN KITCHEN

First and foremost, the truly green kitchen is an energy saving ktichen that uses energy wisely, not wastefully. While there is little disputing the need for us all to cut our consumption of energy in an attempt to cut carbon dioxide emissions and so help to control global warming, there are other steps we can take that can also have a positive effect on the environment.

GREEN MACHINES

Perhaps the well-used advertising slogan 'the appliance of science' should be traded in for a new one for the 1990s — the appliance of *conscience*.

Manufacturers of electrical equipment are responding to environmental concerns by cutting energy consumption of many appliances. Dishwashers, for example, used to have a wattage of 3,000, but now it's possible to buy models consuming just half of that, 1,500 W. Colour TVs *can* have a wattage as low as 40, while others might exceed 150. If you're replacing old appliances or buying new for the first time, it is well worth comparing the wattage on different models.

CFCs AND FRIDGES

Chlorofluorocarbons, or the much more manageable term CFCs, pose two environmental hazards:

● CFCs damage the ozone layer that protects the earth from harmful ultraviolet rays from the sun, and the more ozone is depleted, the greater the threat of skin cancer.
● CFCs contribute to the greenhouse effect and global warming by adding to the gases that are accumulating in the atmosphere.

CFCs are used in fridges and freezers in the home and in shops and factories, too. There are two types of CFCs in fridges. One is used in the cooling system of the fridge or freezer, the other in the insulating foam that keeps the cool air in the cabinet. While in use there is little chance of either type of CFC escaping from the appliance and polluting the atmosphere. The problems begin when an appliance is discarded and dumped. As the fridge or freezer is broken up, both coolant and insulation can be released to the air, letting the CFCs escape.

Manufacturers are already investigating alternatives to both forms of CFCs but at present action is limited to removing the CFCs from discarded appliances. The coolant can, in fact, be recycled, but the insulating foam cannot be reused, so safe ways of disposing of it are being looked at.

If you are buying a fridge or freezer consider the following:

● choose a model with reduced CFC insulation
● buy from a retailer who will recycle the coolant from your old fridge and will monitor eventual disposal of the cabinet
● choose a model with a lower wattage to cut energy consumption
● look out for models where the condenser panel is fitted inside the cabinet of the fridge as this will help to increase the efficiency of the appliance (most condenser panels are at the back of the fridge and when dust accumulates on the panel it works less efficiently) and other energy efficient features, such as a better functioning compressor (cooling system) and temperature-controlled zones in the fridge.

WASHING MACHINES

The major 'green' selling points for washing machines are concerned with energy consumption. The amount of hot water used per load can differ widely and can influence the energy consumption dramatically. Half-load facilities will also help to cut energy use, but generally it's more economical to wait until there is a full load to be washed — unless there is a small amount of washing requiring a special programme, in which case the half-load facility will be economical.

Washer/dryer machines are obviously more expensive to run and use more energy than a washing machine alone. Separate tumble driers also consume comparatively high amounts of electricity, so try to dry washing either outside or near a radiator.

Another environmental aspect of washing is detergent use (see page 37). Some manufacturers claim lower than average detergent consumption on their appliances by reclaiming from waste water or by other specific features unique to their machine.

Look out for the following when choosing a washing machine:

● look out for a half-load facility
● consider spin speed, as the faster the spin speed, the less the need for tumble drying as the clothes emerge drier than from machines with low spin speeds.
● compare wattage — this can vary widely and for a basic machine may be as much as half
● look out for claims about detergent use.

DISHWASHERS

If a family owns a dishwasher it's likely to exceed the running costs of the washing machine, but be less than the cooker and freezer.

Dishwashers are often regarded as expensive luxuries — expensive to buy initially and to run. It's difficult to compare their running costs with the costs of washing-up by hand, but newer models with energy-saving features may well, perform better as well as taking the drudgery out of washing-up. New models may feature more powerful jet sprays to better clean the dishes using less water than before and there may also be economy, quick washes, too.

If you are buying a dishwasher look for the following:

- the wattage — new models may have a wattage half that of conventional machines
- the water consumption — the amount of water required per wash.
- an economy or quick wash facility
- compare detergent use between models.

THE KETTLE

- Keep elements free of scale (mineral deposits from hard water) by regularly descaling them. This will improve the efficiency of the kettle.
- Don't always fill the kettle. If only a small amount of water is required boil just enough, remember to cover the elements, however.
- Plastic jug kettles can save as much as 25 per cent more energy than conventional design kettles.
- If you are using the gas hob, you can save energy by boiling water in a kettle for vegetables then transfering it to the saucepan.

GREEN CLEANERS

Appliance manufacturers have been quick to latch on to consumer interest in domestic detergents and their potential pollution threat. Features such as low-detergent dependence on washing machines and dishwashers are designed to appeal to consumers keen to reduce their use of washing powders, washing-up liquids and the whole army of products that are available for cleaning today's home. Detergent manufacturers have reacted to the growing popularity of 'green' cleaners and now all sorts of powders, cream cleansers, bleaches, toilet cleaners and floor cleaners are available with environmentally friendly claims emblazoned across their packaging.

The key to detergents' link with pollution lies in their make-up. Washing powder was originally based on soap, but because of its low effectiveness in hard-water areas, synthetic detergents were developed — detergent being the active cleaning agent in the product. Most detergents are derived from petrochemicals and although efficient in cleaning dishes and clothes, caused problems through their persistence in the water supply, leading to foaming rivers as suds refused to break up. Legislation was introduced to control the problem and detergents then had to be 80 per cent biodegradable within 19 days — that is they must have broken down during that time.

Manufacturers of 'green' cleaners, however, claim that this is not sufficient and that water pollution can still occur. Total biodegradability is claimed by the new wave manufacturers, even though mass-market companies state that, in practice, their detergents break down quicker than the basic minimum stipulated by law.

Modern cleaners contain other substances in addition to the basic detergent. Large quantities of phosphates may be added to soften the water — washing powder commonly contains as much as 40 per cent phosphate, for example. Phosphates themselves can aggravate water pollution by causing algae to proliferate to such an extent that other forms of water life are deprived of their vital oxygen. An estimated 30 per cent of the total phosphate pollution comes from washing powders — the rest being derived from agro-chemicals. As a result, many manufacturers are reducing phosphate content of washing powder (be wary of phosphate-free claims on washing-up liquid — it never usually contains phosphates anyway!)

Bleaches, brighteners and whiteners, together with enzymes to give 'biological' action, are all added to today's cleaners and, as well as showing poor biodegradability, some of those additives may cause skin rashes and eczema, particularly in young children.

Household cleaners in virtually all categories are now available without these offending ingredients, featuring in their place more acceptable alternatives such as:

- soap or detergents made from vegetable oils in place of petrochemicals
- vinegar instead of chlorine bleach
- essential plant oils in place of synthetic perfumes
- herbs to soften the hands
- unrefined sea salt to stablize products.

These are some of the more common alternatives to conventional cleaners. It is up to the consumer to assess their effectiveness against the benefit to the environment.

AEROSOLS

Detergents are not the only products to start displaying environmentally friendly logos and claims. Aerosols — hairsprays, deodorants, polishes and shaving foam — are all being promoted as such. This is due to an almost complete removal of CFCs from aerosols sold in UK shops.

As explained on page 35, CFCs contribute to global warming and to the destruction of the ozone layer around the planet. CFCs have been used as the main propellant gas in spray cans for years, but following a major campaign by Friends of the Earth that drew public attention to the problem, virtually 90 per cent of UK aerosols are now free of CFCs, using in their place hydrocarbons, which do not pollute. The remaining 10 per cent of aerosols are not on sale to the public, being medical or industrial, so now virtually all aerosols sold in shops are CFC-free.

If you are buying an aerosol, check that the label says as much. If it doesn't, buy a brand that does make the claim — or buy a pump action spray, roll-on or trigger action product. They *may* not be labelled ozone friendly but that's because they were never ozone unfriendly to start with!

PAPER PRODUCTS

Chlorine bleach is widely used industrially as well as in the home, and campaigners have been successful in highlighting the environmental problems that can occur when large quantities of bleach are used in processing paper to produce that bright white we have come to expect. Chlorine bleach is used in the manufacture of many paper products, such as disposable nappies and sanitary protection, and paper cartons for food.

Hazardous dioxins are produced as a by-product of the bleaching process and these create two problems. First, dioxins are present in the waste effluent that is discharged from the factories into waterways. The dioxin problem was first established in Scandinavia where large numbers of paper processing plants are situated. Researchers realized that large numbers of fish were dying in rivers and lakes adjacent to paper plants and established the link with the dioxin pollution from the plant's waste. The second problem area is the potential transfer of dioxins from nappies and sanitary towels into the body and from packaging into food and then into the body. Quite what the risks are is not clear, but in the meantime manufacturers are already responding to consumer fears and are using alternatives to chlorine bleach in the production of paper pulp. That is why many brands of disposable nappies are now labelled with environmentally friendly stickers and logos, but just how ecological these products are is open to debate since they require trees to be felled for their production in the first place and they add to waste disposal problems, too. Conversely they do save on hot water and detergent.

WOOD

In 1988 the UK imported 1.83 million cubic yards (1.4 million cubic metres) of tropical hardwoods, 80 per cent of which ended up being carved into furniture for our kitchen units, lounges and dining rooms. Tropical hardwoods are cheap, hardwearing and attractive, but they might also be taken from virgin areas of the rainforest in countries such as Brazil, South East Asia and Africa.

The controversy over the destruction of the rainforest is well known and buying timber that has been taken from the forest obviously does not help. The alternative is to choose wood that has been taken from a managed plantation where the growth and felling of trees is properly controlled. Friends of the Earth are actively campaigning on this subject and the *Good Wood Guide* explains the issues at stake and lists the sustainable types of tropical timber, giving its 'Good Wood Seal of Approval' to suitable woods.

There are plenty of other types of wood that do not come from such environmentally sensitive areas. Hardwoods grown in temperate regions like our own beech, ash and elm, for example, can also be obtained from acceptable plantations that do not threaten virgin areas of forest. So, before refitting your kitchen, changing your front door or investing in any form of wooden furniture, consider the type of timber from which it is made and where it might have come from.

RECYCLING

Last, but by no means the least important aspect of the green kitchen is recycling. It's appropriate that it comes last on the list because recycling is all about what we do with our rubbish. In most households it simply gets thrown into the bin and taken away by the dustmen, but as concern grows over the use and misuse of vital resources, so does pressure for industry, national and local government and us, the throw-away consumers, to do something about what we are throwing away.

Our dustbins contain a motley collection of boxes, cartons, plastics, glass, tins, newspapers and food scraps. A staggering 70 per cent of Britain's rubbish comes from packaging alone. Isn't it time manufacturers took steps to eliminate some of the unnecessary layers of wrapping or to revive the old-fashioned returnable bottles with refundable deposits? The more packaging that's used on products, the more energy and materials are used in its production and the more land is taken up in landfill sites where our rubbish is dumped.

From the contents of a typical dustbin the following could be salvaged and used again:

● **glass:** in Britain we recycle a meagre 15 per cent of our glass compared to much more impressive figures in all other European countries — Switzerland for example, recycle 55 per cent, Holland 53 per cent and Austria and Belgium both recycle 50 per cent of the glass used. Up to a tenth of household waste is glass and we're so bad at saving it and taking it to the local bottle bank that UK manufacturers actually have to import recycled glass from other countries to meet their needs. Bottle banks are beginning to appear in council and supermarket car parks, but we have a long way to go before we can compare to Holland where there's a bottle bank for every 1,400 people.

● **plastic**: it's unfortunate that of all the common packaging materials, plastic is the least easy to recycle because plastic is being used more and more for packaging our food, drink and toiletries. Plastics are *not* environmentally friendly — they are bulky, accounting for much of the volume of our rubbish and, if burnt, produce unpleasant chemical fumes. There are recyclable bottles available — PET — but as there is virtually no opportunity for the green consumer to hand back the bottles for recycling the chance is wasted. This is obviously an area where much could be done.

● **cans**: Britain manages to recycle a paltry 2 per cent of the cans used nationwide — how come America can recycle 60 per cent of the 75 billion cans used annually? Much more work needs to be done by manufacturers to make it easy for consumers to hand back cans for reuse rather than throwing them away in the refuse. There are some collection points, set up under the 'Save a Can Scheme', which is run by the Can Manufacturers Association, but there are far more collection points required before we can hope to achieve anything like the percentage recycling figure of the States. After all, cans, like glass, account for 10 per cent of domestic rubbish, so the problem is a large one and well worth more effort.

● **paper**: one environmental aspect of paper products has been discussed (see page 39), but the sheer bulk of waste paper thrown away poses a different problem. The more paper we discard, the more trees have to be felled and the more energy has to be used in milling it to the desired result. Paper can be recycled from the home and paper products — newspapers, magazines, writing paper, books, paper tissues, carrier bags the list is almost endless — could all be made from recycled paper, but only 27 per cent of paper in Britain and only a fifth of newspapers and magazines are recycled — what could be easier to collect for recycling?

● **food**: the organic gardener will know that food scraps can be recycled and put to great use in the garden — not as they are, of course, but once they have been composted down on a compost heap or in a covered compost bin together with garden rubbish, grass cuttings and so on. Returning the compost to the soil boosts the fertility of the soil by improving the mineral level, adding humus to improve texture and generally enhancing the condition of the soil. The Henry Doubleday Research Association publish a series of leaflets on this aspect — and others — of organic gardening (see page 153 for address).

The potential environmental benefits of recycling are clear to see and relatively easy to do something positive about. Other environmental problems are not so straightforward, but in all cases the initiative for action is coming from the consumer. It's time the balance was put right, it is time that governments, industry and commerce all set the scene for improving the environment today for tomorrow's enjoyment, before it is too late. We can *all* help — the most simple of actions if repeated the country over, the world over, can make a difference. *You* can make a difference. I dedicated this book to Katy my daughter who, as I finish this book, is just six months old. We must act now to save the environment for the children of today to enjoy tomorrow.

B THE PRACTICE

THE RECIPES

Green cooking is not just about cooking with spinach and cabbage and making salads. Green cooking involves thinking carefully about the food we eat in *all* its aspects — production, preparation and its value to the body that have been outlined in the previous chapters. The essential elements of green cooking are:

● buying organic foods whenever possible, and that includes cereals (rice, wholemeal flour, bread, pasta and so on) and dairy produce as well as fresh fruits and vegetables and an increasing number of 'healthy' prepared foods, e.g. peanut butter, low-sugar jam etc
● buying free-range eggs and, for non-vegetarians, free-range poultry and, sparingly, free-range or organic meat
● avoiding highly processed or refined foods, sugar and salt and restricting the amount of fat and fatty foods we eat
● making more of plant protein foods — cereals, beans, lentils, nuts and seeds — and using animal protein foods — meat, poultry, fish and dairy produce — more sparingly
● using energy wisely not wastefully in the kitchen.

Making these principles part of our everyday living can make a difference, to our own health and to that of the planet.

5 FOOD IN THE RAW

The most environmentally friendly recipes of all must be those that do not require any cooking. They are user friendly, too, because raw fruit and vegetables are likely to contain more vitamin C, as they lose this vitamin in cooking, and vital enzymes. There is something truly energizing about eating crunchy salads of colourful, fresh fruit and vegetables — you can almost *feel* them doing you good! There is no doubt that a salad a day is an excellent recipe for better health. For many, however, the word 'salad' still conjures up visions of limp lettuce, cucumber and tomato. In practice, though, just about any fruit or vegetable can be transformed into a salad, either to be eaten by itself or as an accompaniment to something more substantial.

There are other ways of serving raw food, too. Smooth-textured fromage frais, the thicker, strained Greek-style yogurts and cottage or Ricotta cheese are perfect for serving with raw fruit and vegetables to add a contrasting texture, as well as boosting the protein content of the dish. Ingredients for raw recipes must be carefully prepared and thoroughly cleaned before using and only top-quality ingredients used as poor flavour and condition will not be masked, as they sometimes can be, by cooking. That does not mean that raw recipes lack flavour — on the contrary, as adding fresh herbs and perhaps some spice occasionally can result in a wealth of different flavours.

Unless a recipe calls for food to be prepared in advance, perhaps so flavours can mingle, it is important to prepare the ingredients just before serving. Vitamin C is destroyed when fresh fruit and vegetables are cut and, obviously, the longer the time between cutting and eating, the greater that loss will be. Not only will the food be doing you more good, but the appearance and texture are at their peak then, too.

ORIENTAL SALAD

Serves 4

Imperial/Metric	USA
8 oz/225g mung bean sprouts, washed	4 cups mung bean sprouts, washed
8 oz/225g carrot, scrubbed and cut into ½-in/13-mm matchsticks	1⅓ cups carrot, scrubbed and cut into ½-inch matchsticks
1 large green pepper, deseeded and cut into ½-in/13-mm strips	1 large green sweet pepper, deseeded and cut into ½-inch strips
1 oz/30g blanched almonds, halved lengthways	¼ cup shelled almonds, halved lengthwise
1 oz/30g sesame seeds, lightly toasted	2 tablespoons sesame seeds, lightly toasted
1 tablespoon sunflower oil	1 tablespoon safflower oil
1 teaspoon sesame oil	1 teaspoon sesame oil
2 teaspoons soya sauce	2 teaspoons soy sauce
2 teaspoons cider vinegar	2 teaspoons cider vinegar

1. Put the beansprouts in a bowl.
2. Mix the carrot and the (sweet) pepper with the beansprouts.
3. Add the almonds and sesame seeds to the bowl.
4. Shake the oils, soya sauce and vinegar together in a clean screw-top jar and pour over the salad, tossing it thoroughly. Serve at once.

CAULIFLOWER CRUNCH SALAD

Serves 4

Imperial/Metric	USA
1 small cauliflower, broken into tiny florets	1 small cauliflower, broken into tiny florets
¼ cucumber, cut into 1-in/2.5-cm matchsticks	¼ cucumber, cut into 1-inch matchsticks
2 oz/55g dried apricots, soaked in boiling water for 1 hour, drained and finely shredded	Heaped ⅓ cup dried apricots, soaked in boiling water for 1 hour, drained and finely shredded
4 spring onions, finely sliced diagonally	4 scallions, finely sliced diagonally
2 tablespoons sunflower oil	2 tablespoons safflower oil
2 teaspoons white wine vinegar	2 teaspoons white wine vinegar
2 sprigs fresh tarragon, finely chopped	2 sprigs fresh tarragon, finely chopped

1. Mix the cauliflower, cucumber, apricots and spring onions (scallions) together.

2. Shake together the oil, vinegar and tarragon in a clean screw-top jar.

3. Pour on to the salad, toss thoroughly, then serve at once.

SPINACH SALAD

Serves 2

Imperial/Metric	USA
8 oz/225g fresh, young spinach, washed, stalks discarded, leaves torn into fine shreds	5 cups fresh, young spinach, washed, stems discarded, leaves torn into fine shreds
1 large avocado, really ripe, flesh finely chopped	1 large avocado, really ripe, flesh finely chopped
8 cherry tomatoes	8 cherry tomatoes
1 oz/30g sunflower seeds, toasted	2 tablespoons sunflower seeds, toasted

1. Arrange the spinach on 2 plates.
2. Toss the avocado with the spinach.
3. Arrange the tomatoes on top of the spinach and avocado and scatter the sunflower seeds on top. Serve at once.

CRUNCHY RICE SALAD

Serves 4

Imperial/Metric	USA
6 oz/170g long-grain brown rice	¾ cup long-grain brown rice
8 oz/225g carrot, scrubbed and finely grated	1⅓ cups carrot, scrubbed and finely shredded
2 heaped tablespoons yogurt	2 heaped tablespoons yogurt
1 tablespoon mayonnaise	1 tablespoon mayonnaise
2 oz/55g sunflower seeds, toasted or dry roasted	Heaped ¼ cup sunflower seeds, toasted or dry roasted

1. Put the rice in a saucepan, cover with cold water, bring to the boil, then reduce the heat and simmer for about 20 minutes until the rice is tender.
2. As soon as the rice is cooked, drain, mix with the carrot, yogurt, mayonnaise and sunflower seeds and leave to cool.

CELERY CRUNCH

Serves 4

Imperial/Metric	USA
8 sticks celery, finely sliced	8 celery stalks, finely sliced
4 oz/115g raisins	⅔ cup raisins
4 oz/115g walnuts, coarsely chopped	¾ cup English walnuts, coarsely chopped
2 Cox apples, cored and finely diced	2 sweet dessert apples, cored and finely diced
Juice of ½ lemon, mixed with a little cold water	Juice of ½ lemon, mixed with a little cold water
2 tablespoons natural yogurt	2 tablespoons plain yogurt
2 tablespoons mayonnaise	2 tablespoons mayonnaise
½ teaspoon ground cumin seeds (optional)	½ teaspoon ground cumin seeds (optional)

1. Put the celery in a mixing bowl.
2. Add the raisins and walnuts.
3. Toss the apple in the lemon juice and water, strain off the liquid, then add the apple to the bowl.
4. Whisk in the yogurt and mayonnaise.
5. If liked, add the cumin to the mayonnaise to give a spicy flavour. Serve at once.

WATERCRESS TOSS

Serves 4

Imperial/Metric	USA
1 bunch watercress, washed and trimmed	1 bunch watercress, washed and trimmed
4 oz/115g red cabbage, or 1 small radicchio lettuce, washed and finely shredded	1 cup red cabbage, or 1 small radicchio lettuce, washed and finely shredded
2 oranges, peeled, pith and pips removed, segments halved	2 oranges, peeled, with pith and seeds removed, segments halved
2 spring onions, finely chopped	2 scallions, finely chopped
1 tablespoon sunflower oil	1 tablespoon safflower oil
1 teaspoon cider vinegar	1 teaspoon cider vinegar
Pinch mustard powder	Pinch mustard powder

1. Toss the watercress and red cabbage, or raddicchio, together in a bowl.
2. Add the orange to the bowl.
3. Put the spring onions (scallions) in a screw-top jar with the oil, vinegar and mustard.
4. Shake the dressing vigorously, then pour it over the salad.
5. Toss it all together well and serve at once.

AVOCADO WITH FROMAGE FRAIS

Serves 2

Imperial/Metric	USA
1 large, ripe avocado, halved, stone removed	1 large, ripe avocado, halved and pitted
4 oz/115g fromage frais	½ cup Ricotta cheese

1. Put 1 avocado half on each plate.
2. Scoop the fromage frais (Ricotta) into the cavity and serve — simple but quite delicious!

GREEN BEAN SALAD

Serves 4

Imperial/Metric	USA
2 oz/55g flageolet beans, soaked overnight	⅓ cup flageolet beans, soaked overnight
4 oz/115g wholewheat pasta shells, or spirals	2 cups whole wheat pasta shells, or spirals
6 oz/170g fresh or frozen broad beans	1 cup fava beans
4 spring onions, finely chopped	4 scallions, finely chopped
2 tablespoons sunflower oil	2 tablespoons safflower oil
2 teaspoons cider vinegar	2 teaspoons cider vinegar
1 tablespoon chives, finely chopped	1 tablespoon chives, finely chopped
Freshly ground black pepper	Freshly ground black pepper

1. Put the flageolet beans in fresh water and cook for 1¼-1½ hours, then drain.
2. Meanwhile plunge the pasta into a pan of boiling water and cook for 10-12 minutes until *al dente*.
3. Also cook the broad (fava) beans in a small amount of water until just tender, then drain.
4. Mix the spring onion (scallions), oil, vinegar, chives and pepper in a screw-top jar and, when the beans and pasta are cooked, toss them immediately in it as they will absorb the flavours best at this time.
5. Leave the salad to cool before serving.

GUACAMOLE

Serves 4 as a dip.

Full of flavour, this makes a perfect dip to serve with crudités.

Imperial/Metric	USA
2 ripe tomatoes, skinned and finely chopped	2 ripe tomatoes, skinned and finely chopped
3 sprigs fresh coriander, finely chopped	3 sprigs fresh coriander, finely chopped
2 oz/55g onion, finely chopped	⅓ cup onion, finely chopped
½ green chilli, finely chopped	½ green chili pepper, finely chopped
Juice of ½ lemon, or lime	Juice of ½ lemon, or lime
Freshly ground black pepper	Freshly ground black pepper
1 large, ripe avocado	1 large, ripe avocado

1. Put the tomatoes in a bowl.
2. Add the coriander, onion and chilli (chili pepper), lemon, or lime juice and the pepper to the tomatoes, mix well and leave to stand in the fridge for 1 hour.
3. About 30 minutes before the hour is up, halve the avocado, remove the stone (pit), scoop out the flesh and mash with a fork until it is of a smooth consistency.
4. Beat it into the tomato mixture, then cover until required, but don't leave it for more than 30 minutes as the avocado will start to blacken.

FRESH FRUIT SALAD

Serves 6

Fresh fruit salad is one of those wonderful dishes that can be prepared exactly as you want it, using your favourite fruits or whatever is cheapest and easily available on the day! Serve simply as it is or with a spoonful of yogurt (strained Greek yogurt is a delicious alternative to everyday yogurt) or a scoop of sorbet on really hot summer days.

Imperial/Metric	USA
½ a melon — Galia or Ogen for colour, or Honeydew, or portion of water melon — skinned, seeds removed and diced	½ a melon — Galia or Ogen for colour, or Honeydew or portion of water melon — skinned, seeds removed and diced
½ a pineapple, or 2 peaches, or 2 nectarines, skinned and diced	½ a pineapple, or 2 peaches, or 2 nectarines, skinned and diced
2 large oranges, peeled, pith and seeds removed and diced	2 large oranges, peeled, pith and seeds removed and diced
8 oz/225g seedless grapes, white or black	1½ cups seedless grapes, white or black
3 tablespoons apple juice, preferably freshly pressed, or orange juice	3 tablespoons apple juice, preferably freshly pressed, or orange juice
1 tablespoon Cointreau (optional)	1 tablespoon Cointreau (optional)
2 red-skinned eating apples, cored and finely sliced or diced	2 red-skinned dessert apples, cored and finely sliced or diced
Juice of ½ lemon	Juice of ½ lemon

1. Put the melon, pineapple, or peach, or nectarine, orange and grapes in a large, glass bowl with any juice.
2. Mix all the fruit together with the fruit juice and Cointreau, if using, and chill until just before serving.
3. Toss the apples in the lemon juice before stirring into the bowl. Serve.

R ED FRUIT WHIP

Serves 2

Imperial/Metric	USA
1 lb/455g ripe strawberries, or raspberries	3½ cups ripe strawberries, or raspberries
8 oz/225g Greek strained yogurt	1 cup Greek strained yogurt
2 oz/55g flaked almonds, lightly toasted	½ cup slivered almonds, lightly toasted

1. For a really smooth whip, sieve (strain) the strawberries or raspberries before beating into the yogurt. Alternatively, chop them finely and stir into the yogurt.
2. Divide the whip between two glasses and then scatter the almonds on top.

C ITRUS SPECIAL

Serves 2

Imperial/Metric	USA
¼ or small, Galia or Ogen melon, skinned and diced	¼ or small Galia or Ogen melon, skinned and diced
1 large, or 2 small, oranges, peeled, pith and pips removed, broken into segments	1 large, or 2 small, oranges, peeled, pith and seeds removed, broken into segments
1 grapefruit, peeled, pith and pips removed, broken into segments	1 grapefruit, peeled, pith and seeds removed, broken into segments
Juice of 1 lime	Juice of 1 lime
Clear honey (optional)	Clear honey (optional)

1. Divide the melon between 2 glass dishes and arrange the orange and grapefruit on top.
2. Pour over the lime juice and a little clear honey, if liked, to sweeten.

FRESH FRUIT PLATTER

Serves 2

Imperial/Metric	USA
6 oz/170g fromage frais, or cottage cheese	⅔ cup plus 2 tablespoons Ricotta cheese
2 sticks celery, cut into 3-in/7.5-cm lengths	2 celery stalks, cut into 3-inch lengths
¼ small melon, preferably Ogen or Galia, sliced into segments	¼ small melon, preferably Ogen or Galia, sliced into segments
8 strawberries	8 strawberries
1 peach, sliced into segments	1 peach, sliced into segments
Handful white seedless grapes	Handful white seedless grapes

1. Put half the fromage frais, or cottage cheese (Ricotta), on each plate in a neat mound in the centre.
2. Arrange the celery and fruit around the mound. Serve straight away and eat using the celery and fruit to scoop up the fromage frais, or cottage cheese (Ricotta).

GREEK DELIGHT

Serves 2

Imperial/Metric	USA
8 oz/225g Greek strained yogurt	1 cup Greek strained yogurt
6 oz/170g white seedless grapes	1 heaped cup white seedless grapes
2 ripe pears, cored and finely chopped, or peaches, peeled, stone removed and finely chopped	2 ripe pears, cored and finely chopped, or peaches, peeled, pitted and finely chopped
1 large banana, peeled and sliced	1 large banana, peeled and sliced
1 tablespoon clear Greek honey	1 tablespoon clear Greek honey

1. Divide the yogurt between 2 shallow glass dishes.
2. Divide the fruit between the two bowls, folding it into the yogurt gently.
3. Dribble the honey over the top and serve at once.

USESLI

Makes 2¼ lb/1.15kg

Make a large quantity, store it in an airtight container and serve for special
breakfasts, or indulge yourself every day!

Imperial/Metric	USA
1 lb/450g jumbo oat flakes	4 cups jumbo oat flakes
4 oz/115g rye flakes	1 cup rye flakes
4 oz/115g raisins	⅔ cup raisins
4 oz/115g dried apple rings, chopped	1 cup dried apple rings, chopped
2 oz/55g dried apricots, chopped	½ cup dried apricots, chopped
2 oz/55g dates, chopped	½ cup dates, chopped
2 oz/55g flaked almonds, coarsely chopped	½ cup slivered almonds, coarsely chopped
2 oz/55g hazelnuts, finely chopped	½ cup hazelnuts, finely chopped
¼ teaspoon ground cinnamon	¼ teaspoon ground cinnamon

1. Mix all the ingredients together and store in an airtight container.
2. Serve with skimmed milk, natural yogurt or fruit juice, adding
freshly sliced banana, if liked, for a really nourishing start to the day.

6 FOOD IN A FLASH

If the words 'fast food' conjure up pictures of pizza, burgers and chips, think again. *Fast* food doesn't have to mean *junk* food. There are plenty of wholesome foods that can be prepared in a flash, saving precious resources.

Real fast food saves:

● time — foods that can be prepared and cooked quickly save time spent in the kitchen;

● energy — foods that cook quickly use up less fuel and energy in their preparation;

● and they boost health, too, because quick cooking methods cut down on the loss of heat-sensitive vitamins B and C.

Many fast foods are high in fat. Bought convenience foods and take-away foods contain hidden fat, but if you prepare food at home it's easy to control the amount of fat being used. Both these types of commercial fast food are contain added ingredients of dubious benefit. Processed foods are often labelled with a concoction of additives such as preservatives to prolong shelf-life, colourings to boost appearance and flavour enhancers to do just what their name suggests. Buying foods of this type is also likely to increase your chances of exposure to food poisoning bacteria. The new generation of cook-chill foods that are filling supermarket shelves are potential sources of listeria while take-away foods, which have been sitting around being kept warm for long periods of time, may harbour salmonella. Choosing top-quality ingredients and storing them correctly at home will help you to cut down your exposure to contamination.

HOW TO COOK

The recipes in this section are all prepared, from start to finish, in less than an hour — some in a lot less than that. Cooking time is no more than 40 minutes — some taking as little as 5 minutes — and all are prepared on the hob without the need to use the oven at all. Most recipes require just one ring on the hob, which further saves fuel and, because many are 'one pot' recipes, they save on washing-up, too!

WHAT TO COOK

All the ingredients have undergone the minimum of expensive processing and contain the maximum of nutrients. The recipes are made using a selection of fresh vegetables, wholemeal pasta, nuts, lentils and brown rice. There's a range of soups that are simple to prepare, and which can be cooked ahead and reheated for extra convenience, as well as main-course dishes.

VEGETARIAN PAELLA

Serves 4

Imperial/Metric	USA
1 tablespoon olive oil	1 tablespoon olive oil
4 oz/115g onion, finely chopped	⅔ cup onion, finely chopped
1 clove garlic, crushed	1 clove garlic, minced
6 oz/170g tomatoes, skinned and finely chopped	¾ cup tomatoes, skinned and finely chopped
¼ teaspoon turmeric	¼ teaspoon turmeric
10 oz/285g long-grain brown rice	1¼ cups long-grain brown rice
1¼ pt/710ml water	3½ cups water
1 red pepper, deseeded and sliced into ½-in/13-mm lengths	1 red sweet pepper, deseeded and sliced into ½-inch lengths
8 oz/225g French beans, trimmed and cut into ½-in/13-mm lengths	½ cup string beans, trimmed and cut into ½-inch lengths
2 oz/55g almonds, split and lightly toasted	⅓ cup almonds, split and lightly browned
1 ripe avocado, finely sliced, to garnish	1 ripe avocado, finely sliced, to garnish

1. Heat the oil in a pan, add the onion and garlic and cook gently for 1 minute.
2. Add the tomatoes and turmeric and cook gently for 5 minutes.
3. Stir in the rice, coating the grains, add the water, pepper and beans and bring to the boil.
4. Cover, reduce the heat and simmer for 20-25 minutes, or until the rice is tender and the liquid has been absorbed.
5. Toss the almonds into the pan and serve, garnished with the sliced avocado.

SPEEDY LENTIL SPAGHETTI

Serves 4

This basic sauce can be used to make a meatless version of shepherd's pie — simply top with mashed potato and brown under the grill (broiler).

Imperial/Metric	USA
1 tablespoon olive oil	1 tablespoon olive oil
4 oz/115g onion, finely chopped	⅔ cup onion, finely chopped
1 clove garlic, crushed	1 clove garlic, minced
6 oz/170g carrot, scrubbed and finely diced	1 cup carrot, scrubbed and finely diced
1 teaspoon fresh basil, chopped, or ½ teaspoon dried	1 teaspoon fresh basil, chopped, or ½ teaspoon dried
14 oz/397g tin tomatoes, chopped	14 ounce can tomatoes, chopped
7 oz/200g red lentils, soaked for 1 hour	1 heaped cup red lentils, soaked for 1 hour
1 bay leaf	1 bay leaf
1 red pepper, deseeded and finely chopped	1 red sweet pepper, deseeded and finely chopped
½ pt/285ml water	1⅓ cups water
½ teaspoon vegetable stock concentrate	½ teaspoon vegetable stock concentrate
10 oz/285g wholemeal spaghetti	10 ounces whole wheat spaghetti
Parmesan cheese, finely grated, for garnish (optional)	Parmesan cheese, finely grated, for garnish (optional)

1. Put the oil in a large saucepan, add the onion, garlic and carrot and cook gently for 2 minutes.
2. Stir in the basil, tomatoes, lentils, bay leaf, red (sweet) pepper, water and stock concentrate.
3. Bring to the boil, cover, reduce the heat and simmer for 25 minutes or until the lentils are soft.
4. Meanwhile, have ready a pan of boiling water and shortly before the sauce is finished, cook the spaghetti until it is just tender, then drain it thoroughly.
5. Divide the spaghetti between the 4 plates, then pour the sauce over and, if liked, garnish with the Parmesan cheese.

VEGETABLE SATAY

Serves 4

Imperial/Metric	USA
Marinade	
1 clove garlic, crushed	1 clove garlic, minced
1 tablespoon soya sauce	1 tablespoon soy sauce
1 tablespoon sunflower oil	1 tablespoon safflower oil
½ tablespoon sesame oil	½ tablespoon sesame oil
¾ teaspoon sugar	¾ teaspoon sugar
¾ teaspoon Chinese five spice powder	¾ teaspoon Chinese five spice powder

Vegetables	
2 courgettes, wiped and chopped into ¼-in/7-mm slices	2 zucchini, wiped and chopped into ¼-inch slices
1 small aubergine, diced	1 small eggplant, diced
1 red pepper, deseeded and cut into 1-in/2.5-cm squares	1 red sweet pepper, deseeded and cut into 1-inch squares
1 green pepper, deseeded and cut into 1-in/2.5-cm squares	1 green sweet pepper, deseeded and cut into 1-inch squares
2 small onions, cut into segments	2 small onions, cut into segments

Sauce	
2 oz/55g creamed coconut	⅓ cup creamed coconut
¼ pt/140ml boiling water	⅔ cup boiling water
1 teaspoon ground cumin	1 teaspoon ground cumin
½ green chilli, deseeded and chopped	½ green chili pepper, deseeded and chopped
1 oz/30g onion, finely chopped	2 tablespoons onion, finely chopped
2 cloves garlic, crushed	2 cloves garlic, minced
2 teaspoons sunflower oil	2 teaspoons safflower oil
3 tablespoons peanut butter	3 tablespoons peanut butter
1 teaspoon fresh lemon juice	1 tablespoon fresh lemon juice

1. To make the marinade, mix together all the Marinade ingredients.
2. Thread the vegetables alternately onto 4 skewers (wooden ones look authentic), then brush with the marinade and set to one side.
3. To make the sauce, dissolve the coconut in the boiling water and stir in the cumin.
4. Put the chilli (chili pepper), onion and garlic in a small pan with the oil and heat gently to soften.
5. Put the sauce in a blender or liquidizer, add the peanut butter and lemon juice and blend until fairly smooth.
6. Cook the vegetables on a hot barbecue or under a pre-heated grill (broiler), turning them so they cook on all sides — about 10-15 minutes.
7. Meanwhile, gently heat the sauce and when the vegetables are cooked, spoon the sauce over the kebabs. Serve with rice and a salad.

Variation: Chicken Satay can be prepared by slicing 4 oz/115g chicken breast per person, marinating, threading onto skewers and cooking as above.

NUT BURGERS

Makes 4

Any nuts can be used to make these tasty vegetarian burgers. Buying ready ground nuts saves your time and energy, but is more expensive initially.

Imperial/Metric	USA
3 oz/85g fresh wholemeal breadcrumbs	1½ cups whole wheat bread crumbs
3 oz/85g nuts (walnuts, hazelnuts or brazil nuts are best), ground	⅔ cup nuts (English walnuts, hazelnuts kernels or brazil nuts are best), ground
2 oz/55g onion, finely chopped	⅓ cup onion, finely chopped
½ stick celery, finely chopped	½ celery stalk, finely chopped
2 teaspoons sunflower oil	2 teaspoons safflower oil
3 oz/85g carrot, scrubbed and finely grated	½ cup carrot, scrubbed and finely shredded
2 tablespoons parsley, finely chopped	2 tablespoons parsley, finely chopped
2 tablespoons tomato purée	2 tablespoons tomato paste
1 egg, beaten	1 egg, beaten
1 tablespoon sesame seeds	1 tablespoon sesame seeds
Sunflower oil for frying	Safflower oil for frying

1. Put the breadcrumbs in a mixing bowl, reserving 2 tablespoons for coating later.
2. Mix the nuts with the breadcrumbs.
3. Put the onion and celery in a small pan with the oil and heat gently to soften, without browning.
4. Stir the softened onion and celery into the breadcrumb and nut mixture and add the carrot and parsley.
5. Beat in the tomato purée (paste) and egg to bind the mixture — it should be a fairly stiff texture.
6. Divide the mixture into 4 equal portions and press into burger shapes.
7. Mix the sesame seeds with the reserved breadcrumbs and press them onto the burgers to coat them.
8. Chill the burgers for 15 minutes.

9. Pour some oil into a frying pan (skillet) — just enough to coat the bottom — and heat gently.

10. Fry the burgers for 3-4 minutes each side until golden brown.

11. Drain off any excess oil and serve hot with a salad.

PASTA WITH COURGETTES

Serves 2

Imperial/Metric	USA
1 clove garlic, crushed	1 clove garlic, minced
2 oz/55g onion, finely chopped	⅓ cup onion, finely chopped
1 tablespoon olive oil	1 tablespoon olive oil
1 teaspoon fresh marjoram, chopped, or ½ teaspoon dried	1 teaspoon fresh marjoram, chopped, or ½ teaspoon dried
6 oz/170g button mushrooms, wiped and sliced	2¼ cups button mushrooms, wiped and sliced
1 lb/455g tomatoes, skinned and chopped, or tinned, chopped	2⅔ cups tomatoes, skinned and chopped, or canned
6 oz/170g courgette, cut into 1-in/2.5-cm julienne strips	2 heaped cups zucchini, cut into 1-inch matchsticks
4 oz/115g dried wholemeal tagliatelle, or 8 oz/225g fresh	2 cups dried whole wheat tagliatelle, or 4 cups fresh
Freshly ground black pepper	Freshly ground black pepper
Parmesan cheese, finely grated, for garnish (optional)	Parmesan cheese, finely grated, for garnish (optional)

1. Put the garlic and onion in a pan with the olive oil and heat gently for 2 minutes.

2. Stir in the marjoram and mushrooms and cook for 1 minute.

3. Add the tomatoes and courgette (zucchini), bring to the boil, cover, reduce the heat and simmer for 15 minutes.

4. While the sauce is cooking, cook the pasta until just tender and, just as the sauce is ready, drain the pasta well and toss in the sauce.

5. Season to taste with freshly ground black pepper and serve at once, with the Parmesan cheese sprinkled over, if wished.

CAULIFLOWER AND PASTA MORNAY

Serves 4

Imperial/Metric	USA
4 oz/115g wholemeal pasta shapes	2 cups whole wheat pasta shapes
1 large cauliflower, divided into florets	1 large cauliflower, divided into florets
1½ oz/45g soft vegetable margarine	3 tablespoons soft vegetable margarine
4 oz/115g onion, finely chopped	⅔ cup onion, finely chopped
4 oz/115g button mushrooms, wiped and sliced	1½ cups button mushrooms, wiped and sliced
1 oz/30g unbleached white flour	¼ cup unbleached white flour
½ pt/285ml skimmed milk	1⅓ cups skimmed milk
4 oz/115g farmhouse cheese, e.g., double Gloucester or Cheddar	1 cup hard cheese, e.g., New York Cheddar
Freshly ground black pepper	Freshly ground black pepper
2 tablespoons sunflower seeds	2 tablespoons sunflower seeds

1. Cook the pasta in plenty of boiling water until just tender.

2. Meanwhile, cook the cauliflower in a little water until just tender, drain and reserve the cooking fluid.

3. Melt the margarine over a low heat and stir in the onion, cooking it gently until it is just soft.

4. Add the mushrooms and cook gently until the juices run.

5. Add the flour and beat it in well.

6. Gradually add the milk, beating the sauce to a smooth consistency with the cooking fluid from the cauliflower. The sauce should be pourable but not too thin.

7. Beat in the cheese, reserving a small amount, and season to taste with freshly ground black pepper.

8. Arrange the pasta and cauliflower in a warmed dish and pour over the sauce.

9. Sprinkle sunflower seeds on top with the reserved cheese and pop under a very hot grill (broiler) for a few seconds to melt the cheese. Serve at once.

Variation: Use 1 lb/455g/4 cups leeks in place of the cauliflower.

A TOUCH OF SPICE

Indian recipes make delicious vegetarian meals that prove just as popular with confirmed meat-eaters as they are with vegetarians. Serve a selection of different dishes to provide an impressive — and scrumptious — spread.

HICHIRI

Serves 4

Imperial/Metric	USA
1 tablespoon sunflower oil	1 tablespoon safflower oil
8 oz/225g carrot, scrubbed and finely diced	1⅓ cups carrot, scrubbed and diced
8 oz/225g onion, finely chopped	1⅓ cups onion, finely chopped
1 clove garlic, crushed	1 clove garlic, minced
1 teaspoon ground cumin	1 teaspoon ground cumin
1 teaspoon ground coriander	1 teaspoon ground coriander
½ teaspoon turmeric	½ teaspoon turmeric
Pinch nutmeg	Pinch nutmeg
8 oz/225g long-grain brown rice, or brown basmati rice	1 cup long-grain brown rice, or brown basmati rice
1¾ pt/1 litre water	4½ cups water
5 oz/140g red lentils, soaked for 1 hour and drained	¾ cup red lentils, soaked for 1 hour and drained
¼ teaspoon garam masala	¼ teaspoon garam masala

1. Heat the oil in a large saucepan and stir in the carrots, onion and garlic.
2. Cook gently for 1 minute, then stir in the spices.
3. Cook for 30 seconds, stirring constantly.
4. Add the rice and stir to coat it in the spicy mixture.
5. Add the water and lentils, bring to the boil, cover and reduce the heat.
6. Cook for 30 minutes until tender, turning up the heat to cook off the extra liquid at the end of cooking.
7. Turn off heat and stir in the garam masala just before serving.

CAULIFLOWER AND CASHEW NUT PILAFF

Serves 4

Imperial/Metric	USA
2 tablespoons sunflower oil	2 tablespoons safflower oil
1 teaspoon cumin seeds	1 teaspoon cumin seeds
1 clove garlic, crushed	1 clove garlic, minced
4 oz/115g onion, finely chopped	⅔ cup onion, finely chopped
4 oz/115g carrot, finely chopped	⅔ cup carrot, finely chopped
4 oz/115g potato, diced	⅔ cup potato, diced
½ teaspoon turmeric	½ teaspoon turmeric
10 oz/285g long-grain brown rice	1¼ cups long-grain brown rice
1¼ pt/710ml water	3½ cups water
½ cauliflower, divided into florets	½ cauliflower, divided into florets
4 oz/115g field mushrooms, sliced	1½ cups flat cap mushrooms, sliced
4 oz/115g courgette, sliced	1½ heaped cups zucchini, sliced
½ teaspoon garam masala	½ teaspoon garam masala
6 oz/170g cashew nuts	1⅓ cups cashew nuts
Knob unsalted butter	Knob unsalted butter

1. Heat the oil in a large saucepan.

2. Add the cumin seeds and let them sizzle for one minute.

3. Stir in the garlic, onion, carrot and potato and cook gently for 1 minute.

4. Stir in the turmeric, thoroughly, then add the rice, stirring it so that the grains are coated with the oil mixture.

5. Stir in the water, cauliflower, mushrooms and courgettes (zucchini).

6. Bring to the boil, then cover and simmer for 20-25 minutes until the rice is tender and all the liquid has been absorbed.

7. Turn off the heat and stir in the garam masala.

8. Quickly toss the cashew nuts with the butter in a separate pan and cook until they just begin to turn golden, then add them to the rice mixture and serve at once.

MUSHROOM KORMA

Serves 3-4

Imperial/Metric	USA
2 cloves garlic, chopped	2 cloves garlic, chopped
½-in/13-mm cube root ginger, peeled and chopped	½-inch cube root ginger, peeled and chopped
¼ pt/140ml cold water	⅔ cup cold water
2 tablespoons sunflower oil	2 tablespoons safflower oil
2 oz/55g onion, finely chopped	⅓ cup onion, finely chopped
3 cardamom pods	3 cardamom pods
2 cloves	2 cloves
½-in/13-mm stick cinnamon	½-inch stick cinnamon
¾ teaspoon ground cumin seeds	¾ teaspoon ground cumin seeds
¾ teaspoon ground coriander seeds	¾ teaspoon ground coriander seeds
Pinch turmeric	Pinch turmeric
12 oz/340g button mushrooms, wiped and halved	5¼ cups button mushrooms, wiped and halved
2 oz/55g ground almonds	½ cup ground almonds
¼ pt/140ml single cream	⅔ cup light cream

1. Put the garlic and ginger with the water in a blender or liquidizer and blend until smooth.

2. Put the oil in a large heavy-based saucepan and heat gently, then add the onion and the spices and sauté gently for 2 minutes, stirring to mix the ingredients thoroughly.

3. Add the mushrooms and coat in the spicy mixture.

4. Add the garlic, ginger and water mixture to the pan and bring to the boil, then reduce the heat and simmer for 5 minutes.

5. Stir in the ground almonds, mixing them in thoroughly.

6. Stir in the cream, bring gently to the boil, then immediately reduce the heat and simmer very gently for 30 minutes, watching it to make sure the mixture doesn't boil over or curdle.

7. Remove the cinnamon stick, cloves and cardamom pods and serve.

SPICED CHICKPEAS WITH POTATOES

Serves 3

Imperial/Metric	USA
2 tablespoons sunflower oil	2 tablespoons safflower oil
1 dried red chilli, or 1 fresh green chilli, finely chopped	1 dried red chili pepper, or 1 fresh green chili pepper, finely chopped
1 teaspoon ground cumin seeds	1 teaspoon ground cumin seeds
1 teaspoon ground coriander seeds	1 teaspoon ground coriander seeds
¼ teaspoon cayenne pepper	¼ teaspoon cayenne pepper
Pinch turmeric	Pinch turmeric
4 oz/115g onion, finely chopped	⅔ cup onion, finely chopped
2 cloves garlic, finely chopped	2 cloves garlic, finely chopped
½-in/13-mm cube root ginger, peeled and grated	½-inch cube root ginger, peeled and shredded
8 oz/225g potato, scrubbed and diced	1¼ cups potato, scrubbed and diced
14 oz/397g tin tomatoes, chopped	14 ounce can tomatoes, chopped
14 oz/397g tin chickpeas, or 7 oz/200g dried, soaked overnight, then cooked	14 ounce can garbanzos, or 1 heaped cup dried, soaked overnight, then cooked
¼ teaspoon garam masala	¼ teaspoon garam masala

1. Heat the oil in a heavy-based saucepan.
2. Stir in the spices and mix well.
3. Add the onion, garlic and ginger and sauté gently for 2 minutes.
4. Stir in the potato and cook for 2 more minutes.
5. Add the tomatoes and bring to the boil, then reduce the heat and simmer for 15 minutes.
6. Stir in the chickpeas (garbanzos) and simmer for 15 more minutes.
7. Stir in the garam masala, turn off the heat and let the pan stand for 5 minutes to let the flavours mingle before serving.

SPICY VEGETABLE PILAFF

Serves 4

Imperial/Metric	USA
3 tablespoons sunflower oil	3 tablespoons safflower oil
4 oz/115g cashew nuts, or blanched almonds	¾ cup cashew nuts, or blanched almonds
2 oz/55g sultanas	⅓ cup golden seedless raisins
4 oz/115g onion, finely chopped	⅔ cup onion, finely chopped
8 oz/225g carrot, scrubbed and finely diced	1¼ cups carrot, scrubbed and finely diced
½ teaspoon cumin seeds	½ teaspoon cumin seeds
¼ teaspoon turmeric	¼ teaspoon turmeric
8 oz/225g long-grain brown rice, or brown basmati rice	1 cup long-grain brown rice, or brown basmati rice
1 pt/570ml water	2½ cups water
4 oz/115g frozen peas	⅔ cup frozen peas
½ teaspoon garam masala	½ teaspoon garam masala

1. Heat the oil in a large heavy-based saucepan and add the nuts and sultanas (golden seedless raisins).
2. Cook for 1-2 minutes until the nuts begin to turn golden.
3. Remove the nuts and sultanas (golden seedless raisins) using a slotted spoon and set aside.
4. Add the onion, carrot, cumin and turmeric to the oil, stirring thoroughly, and cook for 2 minutes.
5. Stir in the rice, coating the grains thoroughly in the spicy mixture.
6. Add the water, bring to the boil, then reduce the heat and simmer for 20 minutes.
7. Stir in the peas and continue cooking until the rice is tender and all the liquid has been absorbed.
8. Stir in the garam masala, turn off the heat and let it stand for 5 minutes to let the flavours infuse, then serve at once, garnished with the nuts and sultanas (golden seedless raisins).

SPEEDY ORIENTAL MASTERPIECES

Chinese cooking is quick — the only time-consuming part is the preparation of the ingredients — *and* stir-frying preserves nutrients and flavour, too, for the best of both worlds.

Serves 4

Imperial/Metric	USA
1 tablespoon sunflower oil	1 tablespoon safflower oil
1 teaspoon sesame oil	1 teaspoon sesame oil
1 lb/450g fresh broccoli, cut into small florets with 1-in/2.5-cm stalk	4 cups fresh broccoli, cut into small florets with 1-inch stem
4 oz/115g mange-tout, trimmed	4 ounces snow peas, trimmed
4 spring onions, finely sliced diagonally	4 scallions, finely sliced diagonally
4 oz/115g mung beansprouts, washed	4 ounces mung bean sprouts, washed
2 tablespoons water	2 tablespoons water
2 teaspoons light soya sauce	2 teaspoons light soy sauce

1. Heat the oils in a wok or large frying pan (skillet), add the broccoli and mange-tout (snow peas) and stir-fry for 2 minutes.
2. Add the water and soya sauce and cook for 2 more minutes.
3. Stir in the spring onions (scallions) and beansprouts and cook for 2 more minutes, then serve at once.

TOFU CHOW MEIN

Serves 4

Imperial/Metric	USA
8 oz/225g tofu, cut into 1-in/2.5-cm cubes	1 cup tofu, cut into 1-inch cubes
1 teaspoon rice wine, or dry sherry	1 teaspoon rice wine, or dry sherry
3 teaspoons soya sauce	3 teaspoons soy sauce
8 oz/225g egg noodles	1½ heaped cups egg noodles
2 tablespoons sunflower oil	2 tablespoons safflower oil
2 teaspoons sesame oil	2 teaspoons sesame oil
1 clove garlic, crushed	1 clove garlic, minced
1 lb/455g button mushrooms, wiped and halved	8 cups button mushrooms, wiped and halved
2 tablespoons water	2 tablespoons water
2 spring onions, finely sliced diagonally	2 scallions, finely sliced diagonally

1. Put the tofu cubes into a bowl, pour over the rice wine, or sherry, and 1 teaspoon of the soya sauce, mix and leave to marinate for at least 10 minutes.

2. Plunge the noodles into boiling water and cook as directed on the packet.

3. Drain and put them in a bowl of cold water while you cook the rest of the dish.

4. Heat the oils in a wok or large frying pan (skillet) and add the tofu, marinade and garlic, tossing them all together.

5. Stir in the mushrooms, the remaining soya sauce and the water and heat briskly, stirring, for 4 minutes.

6. Drain the noodles and stir into the pan, mixing in well.

7. Add the spring onions (scallions), cook for 2 more minutes to heat the noodles, then serve at once.

FRIED RICE

Serves 4

Imperial/Metric	USA
6 oz/170g long-grain brown rice	⅔ cup long-grain brown rice
1 tablespoon sunflower oil	1 tablespoon safflower oil
4 oz/115g peas, cooked	⅔ cup peas, cooked
2 eggs, beaten	2 eggs, beaten
4 oz/115g mung beansprouts, washed	2 cups mung bean sprouts, washed
2 spring onions, trimmed and finely chopped	2 scallions, trimmed and finely chopped

1. Put the rice in a pan of cold water and bring to the boil, then cover, reduce the heat and simmer until the rice is just tender (about 20 minutes).

2. Drain the rice and set aside (the rice should be quite cold for best results so remember to cook the rice at least 1 hour before serving the meal).

3. Heat the oil in a wok or large frying pan (skillet) and stir in the rice, stirring it briskly to coat it in the oil.

4. Add the peas and, cook for 1 minute.

5. Now quickly stir in the egg and the beansprouts and continue to cook and stir until the egg has solidified.

6. Stir in the spring onions (scallions) and serve at once.

CHINESE MIXED VEGETABLES

Serves 4

Imperial/Metric	USA
1 tablespoon sunflower oil	1 tablespoon safflower oil
6 oz/170g carrot, scrubbed and cut into 1½-in/4-cm matchsticks	1 cup carrot, scrubbed and cut into 1½-inch matchsticks
1 large red pepper, deseeded and cut into 1½-in/4-cm strips	1 large red sweet pepper, deseeded and cut into 1½-inch strips
4 oz/115g baby corn on the cob, or courgette finely sliced diagonally	1½ cups baby corn on the cob, or zucchini finely sliced diagonally
2 teaspoons soya sauce	2 teaspoons soy sauce
2 tablespoons cold water	2 tablespoons cold water
8 oz/225g Chinese leaves, shredded	2 cups Chinese leaves, coarsely chopped
2 spring onions, finely sliced diagonally	2 scallions, finely sliced diagonally

1. Heat the oil in a wok or large frying pan (skillet) and stir in the carrot.

2. Cook it for 1 minute, stirring, before adding the (sweet) pepper, baby corn, or courgette (zucchini) and soya sauce, then stir-fry for 2 more minutes.

3. Stir in the water and Chinese leaves and cook for 2 more minutes, then stir in the spring onions (scallions) and serve at once.

SUPER SOUPS!

Home-made soup is one of the most versatile of dishes. Equally good for an informal light lunch or for a starter to begin a more formal meal, soups present the perfect opportunity to use cheap pulses, in-season vegetables and all manner of 'green' ingredients.

Some soups can be cooked in a flash, and those that need more lengthy cooking — to soften beans or lentils for instance — can be made in large quantities in advance and frozen for later use. (These can be cooked more quickly and with less fuel consumption in a pressure cooker.) The microwave will reheat soup very successfully just in the chosen serving bowl to save on time and energy.

CORN CHOWDER

Serves 4

Imperial/Metric	USA
1 oz/30g unsalted butter, or 1 tablespoon sunflower oil	2 tablespoons unsalted butter, or 1 tablespoon safflower oil
4 oz/115g onion, finely chopped	⅔ cup onion, finely chopped
8 oz/225g potato, scrubbed and diced	1⅓ cups potato, scrubbed and diced
¾ pt/425ml vegetable, or chicken, stock	2 cups vegetable, or chicken, stock
12 oz/340g sweetcorn	2 cups sweetcorn
1 pt/570ml milk (full fat gives a creamier taste)	2½ cups milk (full fat gives a creamier taste)
Freshly ground black pepper	Freshly ground black pepper

1. Melt the butter, or heat the oil, in a large saucepan.
2. Stir in the onion and cook for 2 minutes without browning it.
3. Add the potato and cook for 1 more minute.
4. Add the stock and cook for 10 minutes, simmering gently.
5. Stir in the sweetcorn and milk, bring to the boil, then reduce the heat to very low and simmer gently for 10 more minutes.
6. Season to taste with freshly ground black pepper and serve.

STILTON AND CELERY SOUP

Serves 3, generously

The ideal way of using up leftover pieces of Stilton or other strong-flavoured blue cheese.

Imperial/Metric	USA
8 oz/225g celery, finely chopped	1⅓ cups celery, finely chopped
4 oz/115g onion, finely chopped	⅔ cup onion, finely chopped
¾ oz/20g unsalted butter, or 1½ tablespoons sunflower oil	1½ tablespoons unsalted butter, or 1½ tablespoons safflower oil
1¼ pt/710ml water, plus ½ teaspoon vegetable stock concentrate, or 1¼ pt/710ml vegetable stock	3½ cups water, plus ½ teaspoon vegetable stock concentrate, or 3½ cups vegetable stock
1 bay leaf	1 bay leaf
3 oz/85g Stilton, crumbled finely	½ cup Stilton, crumbled finely
2 tablespoons fromage frais	2 tablespoons Ricotta
2 tablespoons skimmed milk	2 tablespoons skimmed milk
Freshly ground black pepper	Freshly ground black pepper

1. Put the celery and onion with the butter, or oil, in a large suacepan and sweat gently on a low heat, covered, for 5-7 minutes.
2. Add the water and stock concentrate, or stock, and the bay leaf.
3. Bring to the boil, then reduce the heat and simmer for 20 minutes until the celery is soft.
4. Remove the bay leaf and liquidize the soup in a liquidizer or blender.
5. Put the Stilton into a bowl and beat in the fromage frais (Ricotta) and milk, mixing it to a smooth purée.
6. Whisk the purée into the liquidized soup, away from the heat.
7. When it is thoroughly mixed in, return the soup to the saucepan, reheat it gently without boiling and season to taste with freshly ground black pepper. Garnish with a few celery leaves.

COUNTRY VEGETABLE SOUP

Serves 4

Imperial/Metric	USA
1 tablespoon olive oil	1 tablespoon olive oil
1 leek, trimmed and sliced	1 leek, trimmed and sliced
6 oz/170g carrot, scrubbed and diced	1 cup carrot, scrubbed and diced
6 oz/170g swede, or parsnip, peeled and diced	1 cup rutabaga, or parsnip, peeled and diced
6 oz /170g potato, scrubbed and diced	1 cup potato, scrubbed and diced
1 teaspoon fresh marjoram, or oregano, chopped, or ½ teaspoon dried	1 teaspoon fresh marjoram, or oregano, chopped, or ½ teaspoon dried
14 oz/397g tin tomatoes, chopped	14 ounce can tomatoes, chopped
1¼ pt/710ml water	3½ cups water
½ teaspoon vegetable stock concentrate	½ teaspoon vegetable stock concentrate
1 bay leaf	1 bay leaf
2 oz/50g cabbage, finely shredded, or frozen peas, or frozen sweetcorn	½ cup cabbage, finely chopped, or frozen peas, or frozen sweetcorn
Freshly ground black pepper	Freshly ground black pepper

1. Heat the oil in a large saucepan.
2. Stir in the leek, carrot, swede (rutabaga), or parsnip, potato and marjoram, or oregano and heat together for 1 minute.
3. Add the tomatoes, water, stock concentrate and bay leaf, bring to the boil and cook for 30 minutes.
4. Stir in the cabbage, or peas, or sweetcorn, and cook for 5 more minutes.
5. Season to taste with freshly ground black pepper and serve.

POTATO AND BARLEY BROTH

Serves 4

Imperial/Metric	USA
4 oz/115g onion, finely chopped	⅔ cup onion, finely chopped
1 stick celery, finely chopped	1 celery stalk, finely chopped
12 oz/340g potato, scrubbed and diced	2 cups potato, scrubbed and diced
2 tablespoons sunflower oil	2 tablespoons safflower oil
1 heaped tablespoon wholemeal flour	1 heaped tablespoon whole wheat flour
2½ pts/1.4 litres water	1½ quarts water
½ teaspoon vegetable stock concentrate	½ teaspoon vegetable stock concentrate
4 oz/115g pearl barley	½ cup pot barley
1 bay leaf	1 bay leaf
Freshly ground black pepper	Freshly ground black pepper
2 tablespoons fresh parsley, chopped, to garnish	2 tablespoons chopped parsley, to garnish

1. Put the onion, celery and potato with the oil in a large saucepan.

2. Heat gently for 2 minutes without browning.

3. Stir in the flour, mixing thoroughly.

4. Gradually add the water and stock concentrate and let the mixture come slowly to the boil.

5. Add the barley and bay leaf, cover, reduce the heat and simmer for 40-50 minutes until the barley is tender.

6. Season to taste with freshly ground black pepper, pour into warmed soup bowls, garnish with the parsley and serve with chunky pieces of wholemeal bread.

COUNTRY MUSHROOM SOUP

Serves 4

A warming, satisfying soup.

Imperial/Metric	USA
¾ oz/20g unsalted butter, or 1 tablespoon sunflower oil	1½ tablespoons unsalted butter, or 1 tablespoon safflower oil
1 large leek, finely chopped	1 large leek, finely chopped
½ stick celery, finely chopped	½ celery stalk, finely chopped
8 oz/225g potato, scrubbed and finely diced	1⅓ cups potato, scrubbed and finely diced
10 oz/285g button or field mushrooms, wiped and finely chopped	3¾ cups button or flat cap mushrooms, wiped and finely chopped
Sprig fresh thyme, chopped, or ¼ teaspoon dried	Sprig fresh thyme, chopped, or ¼ teaspoon dried
1 pt/570ml skimmed milk	2½ cups skimmed milk
¾ pt/425ml water	2 cups water
1 teaspoon vegetable stock concentrate	1 teaspoon vegetable stock concentrate
1 bay leaf	1 bay leaf
Freshly ground black pepper	Freshly ground black pepper

1. Melt the butter in a large saucepan and stir in the leek, celery and potato and sweat gently for 5 minutes without browning them.
2. Stir in the mushrooms and thyme and cook for 2 more minutes.
3. Add the milk, water, vegetable stock concentrate and bay leaf and bring to the boil.
4. Reduce the heat and cook slowly for 25 minutes until the vegetables are tender.
5. Remove the bay leaf, liquidize the soup in a liquidizer or blender, return it to the saucepan, reheat it, then season to taste with freshly ground black pepper and serve.

SPINACH AND LENTIL SOUP

Serves 3

Imperial/Metric	USA
2 oz/55g onion, finely chopped	⅓ cup onion, finely chopped
1 clove garlic, crushed	1 clove garlic, minced
1 tablespoon sunflower oil	1 tablespoon safflower oil
⅛ teaspoon turmeric	⅛ teaspoon turmeric
¼ teaspoon ground cumin	¼ teaspoon ground cumin
¼ teaspoon ground coriander	¼ teaspoon ground coriander
Pinch cayenne pepper	Pinch cayenne pepper
2 oz/55g green or brown whole lentils, soaked for 1 hour	⅓ cup green or brown whole lentils, soaked for 1 hour
1½ oz/45g creamed coconut	2½ tablespoons creamed coconut
1½ pt/850ml water	3¾ cups water
6 oz/170g frozen spinach, cooked and finely chopped	⅔ cup frozen spinach, cooked and finely chopped

1. Put the onion and garlic in a pan with the oil and cook gently for 1 minute.

2. Add the turmeric, cumin, coriander and cayenne pepper and stir in well.

3. Add the lentils, creamed coconut and water and bring to the boil.

4. Reduce the heat and simmer for 45 minutes.

5. Stir in the spinach and cook for 15 more minutes or until the lentils are quite soft, then serve at once.

CARROT AND TOMATO SOUP

Serves 4

Omit the pasta shapes and, at the end of cooking, liquidize the soup if you prefer a smooth texture.

Imperial/Metric	USA
1 tablespoon olive oil	1 tablespoon olive oil
1 clove garlic, crushed (optional)	1 clove garlic, minced (optional)
½ stick celery, finely chopped	½ celery stalk, finely chopped
4 oz/115g onion, finely chopped	⅔ cup onion, finely chopped
12 oz/340g carrot, scrubbed and finely grated	2 cups carrot, scrubbed and finely shredded
2×14 oz/397g tins tomatoes, chopped	2×14 ounce can tomatoes, chopped
¾ pt/425ml water	2 cups water
½ teaspoon vegetable stock concentrate	½ teaspoon vegetable stock concentrate
1 teaspoon fresh basil, chopped, or ½ teaspoon dried	1 teaspoon fresh basil, chopped, or ½ teaspoon dried
2 oz/55g wholewheat pasta shells	1 cup whole wheat pasta shells
Freshly ground black pepper	Freshly ground black pepper
Parmesan cheese, finely grated, to garnish (optional)	Parmesan cheese, finely grated, to garnish (optional)

1. Heat the oil in a large saucepan, stir in the garlic, if using, celery and onion and sweat gently for 3 minutes.
2. Stir in the carrot, tomatoes, water, vegetable stock concentrate and basil and bring to the boil.
3. Reduce the heat and simmer for 20 minutes.
4. Stir in the pasta and cook for 8-10 more minutes until tender.
5. Season to taste with freshly ground black pepper and serve, garnished with the Parmesan, if liked.

7 PLANT PERFECTION

Eating 'green' means eating more plant foods. That doesn't just mean vegetables and fruits, it means making more of plant foods generally. Many of these are rich in protein and have tended to be overlooked because meat, fish and poultry have — for us in the western world at any rate — become more widely available and affordable. Foods such as grains, nuts, seeds and the pulses (legumes), such as beans and lentils, are considerably cheaper sources of protein than meat and surprisingly tasty, versatile ingredients to cook with. It is important, however, to mix these different plant protein foods together (mixing a grain with a bean or nut or seed, for example) to make the best use of the protein. Alternatively, eating a plant protein food with some dairy produce or other animal protein at the same meal will also provide you with a complete protein combination (see Chapter 1).

Plant protein foods do more for you than just provide protein, they are also good sources of vitamins and minerals and of dietary fibre, particularly the pulses (legumes) and whole grains that have not been refined, removing vital fibre. These foods are generally lower in fat than animal foods, an exception being nuts, which are high in fat, but the fat that is present is less saturated than that found in red meats and dairy produce.

WHAT TO COOK

Most of the recipes in this section are main course vegetarian dishes. There's a selection of warming winter casseroles that can be cooked in the oven, on the hob or in a pressure cooker, and lighter, year-round dishes such as pies, stuffed vegetables and other grain, nut, pulse (legume) and pasta dishes. Stuffed vegetables look attractive and, although sometimes slightly fiddly to prepare, can be made in advance and then baked when required. Stuffings of breadcrumbs, nuts and grains add extra protein to the dish and blend well with different herbs.

SAVOURY CABBAGE ROLLS

Serves 4

Imperial/Metric	USA
12 good-sized cabbage leaves (Savoy or Hispi)	12 good-sized cabbage leaves
6 oz/170g cracked wheat	1 cup cracked wheat
4 oz/115g button mushrooms, wiped and finely chopped	1½ cups button mushrooms, wiped and finely chopped
Knob butter, unsalted	Knob butter, unsalted
4 spring onions, chopped	4 scallions, chopped
3 oz/85g flaked almonds, chopped	¾ cup slivered almonds, chopped
½ teaspoon fresh thyme, or ¼ teaspoon dried	½ teaspoon fresh thyme, or ¼ teaspoon dried
Freshly ground black pepper	Freshly ground black pepper
2 fl oz/60ml vegetable stock	¼ cup vegetable stock

1. Cut across the base of the cabbage leaves and discard the tough stem.

2. Blanch the leaves in two batches, plunging them into a pan of boiling water for 1 minute, then drain well.

3. Place the cracked wheat in a pan with enough cold water to cover and bring to the boil. Reduce the heat, simmer for 5-8 minutes until soft, then drain thoroughly.

4. Place the mushrooms in a covered pan with the butter and cook on a low heat until the juices run.

5. Heat the oven to 400°F/200°C/Gas Mark 6.

6. Mix the cracked wheat with the cooked mushrooms, spring onions (scallions), almonds and thyme and season to taste with black pepper.

7. Place a good tablespoon of the mixture across the centre of each cabbage leaf. Fold in the sides, then fold in the stem end of the leaf and roll up, not too tightly. Arrange the rolls in a shallow ovenproof dish, smooth side uppermost so they stay rolled up, then pour over the stock, cover and bake for 20-25 minutes.

NUT AND MUSHROOM BAKE

Serves 4

Imperial/Metric	USA
4 oz/115g onion, finely chopped	⅔ cup onion, finely chopped
½ stick celery, finely sliced	½ celery stalk, finely sliced
1 tablespoon olive oil	1 tablespoon olive oil
12 oz/340g button mushrooms, wiped and sliced	4¼ cups button mushrooms, wiped and sliced
14 oz/397g tin tomatoes, chopped	14 ounce can tomatoes, chopped
½ teaspoon fresh thyme, or ¼ teaspoon dried	½ teaspoon fresh thyme, or ¼ teaspoon dried
1 bay leaf	1 bay leaf

Topping

4 oz/115g walnuts, ground or finely chopped	¾ cup English walnuts, ground or finely chopped
4 oz/115g fresh wholemeal breadcrumbs	2 cups fresh whole wheat bread crumbs
1 egg, beaten	1 egg, beaten
2 tablespoons sunflower seeds	2 tablespoons sunflower seeds

1. Put the onion, celery and oil in a pan and heat gently for 1 minute.

2. Stir in the mushrooms and coat in the oil.

3. Add the tomatoes, thyme and bay leaf, bring to the boil, cover and simmer for 10 minutes.

4. Meanwhile, heat the oven to 375°F/190°C/Gas Mark 5 and make the topping.

5. Mix the walnuts with the breadcrumbs.

6. When the sauce is ready, pour it into 4 individual serving dishes or 1 large dish.

7. Mix the egg with the nut and breadcrumb mixture to bind it very lightly.

8. Crumble the topping onto the dishes and sprinkle the sunflower seeds on top, then bake for 15 minutes until the topping has lightly browned.

BAKED PEPPERS

Serves 4

This stuffing mixture can also be used for courgettes (zucchini). Why not choose small, different coloured (sweet) peppers, stuff a selection, arrange them on a platter and each person can choose which colour they want to eat!

Imperial/Metric	USA
4 good-sized broad peppers, each about 6 oz/170g	4 good-sized sweet bell peppers, each 6 ounces
2 oz/55g onion, finely chopped	⅓ cup onion, finely chopped
Clove garlic, crushed (optional)	Clove garlic, minced (optional)
2 teaspoons sunflower oil	2 teaspoons safflower oil
6 oz/170g long-grain brown rice	¾ cup long-grain brown rice
¾ pt/425ml water	2 cups water
¼ teaspoon vegetable stock concentrate	¼ teaspoon vegetable stock concentrate
4 oz/115g carrot, scrubbed and coarsely grated	⅔ cup carrot, scrubbed and coarsely shredded
3 oz/85g sweetcorn	½ cup sweetcorn
1 tablespoon tomato purée	1 tablespoon tomato paste
½ teaspoon fresh marjoram, or ¼ teaspoon dried	½ teaspoon fresh marjoram, or ¼ teaspoon dried
2 tablespoons sesame seeds	2 tablespoons sesame seeds
Freshly ground black pepper	Freshly ground black pepper
4 oz/115g Mozzarella cheese, finely sliced, or farmhouse Cheddar, grated	4 ounces Mozzarella cheese, finely sliced, or 1 cup Monterey Jack, shredded

1. Pre-heat the oven to 375°F/190°C/Gas Mark 5.
2. Cut a slice from the top of each (sweet) pepper and scoop out the ribs and seeds.
3. Place the garlic, if using, and oil in a flameproof casserole dish and heat gently for 1 minute.
4. Stir in the rice, coating the grains.
5. Add the water and stock concentrate and bring to the boil.
6. Cover and bake in the oven for about 20 minutes, or until the rice is tender.

7. Meanwhile, blanch the (sweet) peppers by plunging them into boiling water for 1 minute.

8. Drain them thoroughly and arrange in an ovenproof dish, open tops uppermost.

9. When the rice is ready, stir in the carrot, sweetcorn, tomato purée (paste), marjoram and sesame seeds and season to taste with freshly ground black pepper.

10. Divide the mixture between the 4 (sweet) peppers, pressing it well into each one.

11. Place the sliced or sprinkle the grated, cheese on top of each pepper.

12. Spoon a little water around the base of the (sweet) peppers and bake for 20 minutes. Serve with a side salad and fresh bread.

Note: If using courgettes (zucchini), cut out a wedge along each one, scoop out and chop the flesh and add it to the cooked rice mixture. The courgette (zucchini) shells should be blanched in the same way as the (sweet) peppers before stuffing.

A LMOND ROAST

Serves 6

Bake this tasty savoury in a ring mould (tube pan) for an attractive change and fill the centre with a lovely fresh salad or a cooked vegetable.

Imperial/Metric	USA
2 oz/55g onion, finely chopped	⅓ cup onion, finely chopped
1 stick celery, finely chopped	1 celery stalk, finely chopped
2 teaspoons olive oil	2 teaspoons olive oil
6 oz/170g carrot, scrubbed and grated	1 cup carrot, scrubbed and shredded
8 oz/225g button mushrooms, wiped and finely chopped	2¼ cups button mushrooms, wiped and finely chopped
8 oz/225g ground almonds	2 cups ground almonds
8 oz/225g fresh wholemeal breadcrumbs	4 cups fresh whole wheat bread crumbs
1 tablespoon lemon rind, finely grated	1 tablespoon lemon rind, finely shredded
1 tablespoon fresh parsley, finely chopped	1 tablespoon fresh parsley, finely chopped
1 tablespoon fresh thyme, or ½ teaspoon dried	1 teaspoon fresh thyme, or ½ teaspoon dried
3 eggs, beaten	3 eggs, beaten
Freshly ground black pepper	Freshly ground black pepper

1. Pre-heat the oven to 375°F/190°C/Gas Mark 5.
2. Line and lightly oil a 2 lb/900g loaf tin (pan) or an 8-in/20.5-cm ring mould (tube pan).
3. Put the onion and celery in a pan with the olive oil and heat gently until softened.
4. Remove from the heat and pour into a large mixing bowl with the carrot, mushrooms, almonds and breadcrumbs.
5. Mix together thoroughly, then stir in the lemon, parsley and thyme.
6. Mix the eggs into the dry ingredients until it binds to a soft texture.
7. Season lightly with freshly ground black pepper, then pile into the prepared tin (pan) and press down firmly.
8. Smooth the top, cover with foil and bake in the centre of the oven for

35 minutes, then remove the cover and bake for a further 10 minutes to brown the top. Serve hot or cold.

COURGETTES STUFFED WITH PINE KERNELS

Serves 4

Imperial/Metric	USA
4 good-sized courgettes, each about 6 oz/170g	4 good-sized zucchini, each about 6 ounces
4 oz/115g onion, finely chopped	⅔ cup onion, finely chopped
1 tablespoon olive oil	1 tablespoon olive oil
12 oz/340g tomatoes, skinned and chopped	2⅛ cups tomatoes, skinned and chopped
4 oz/115g pine kernels	¾ cup pine kernels
½ teaspoon fresh marjoram, or ¼ teaspoon dried	½ teaspoon fresh marjoram, or ¼ teaspoon dried
Freshly ground black pepper	Freshly ground black pepper
4 tablespoons water	¼ cup water

1. Cut a wedge along the length of each courgette (zucchini), scoop out the flesh and chop it finely.
2. Cook the onion gently in the olive oil with the chopped courgette (zucchini) for 2 minutes.
3. Stir in the tomatoes and cook for 5 minutes.
4. Remove from the heat and stir in the pine kernels and marjoram and season to taste with freshly ground black pepper.
5. Heat the oven 375°F/190°C/Gas Mark 5.
6. Blanch the courgette (zucchini) 'shells' by plunging them into boiling water for 1 minute, then drain them and arrange in a shallow ovenproof dish.
7. Divide the stuffing between the courgettes (zucchini), spoon the water into the base of the dish, cover and bake for 25 minutes. Serve with Oven-baked Rice (see page 105).

OATY VEGETABLE PIE

Serves 3-4

Imperial/Metric	USA
4 oz/115g wholemeal flour	1 cup whole wheat flour
2 oz/55g rolled oats	½ cup rolled oats
3 oz/85g soft vegetable margarine	⅓ cup soft vegetable margarine
Cold water to mix	Cold water to mix

Filling

2 oz/55g onion, chopped	⅓ cup onion, chopped
1 tablespoon sunflower oil	1 tablespoon safflower oil
6 oz/170g carrot, scrubbed and diced	1 cup carrot, scrubbed and diced
6 oz/170g swede, peeled and diced	1 cup rutabaga, peeled and diced
6 oz/170g potato, scrubbed and diced	1 cup potato, scrubbed and diced
¼ teaspoon ground cumin	¼ teaspoon ground cumin
Pinch ground turmeric	Pinch ground turmeric
1 tablespoon wholemeal flour	1 tablespoon whole wheat flour
8 fl oz/240ml vegetable stock	1 cup vegetable stock

1. Put the flour and oats in a mixing bowl and rub (cut) in the margarine.

2. Put in the fridge to rest (stand) while making the filling.

3. Sauté the onion in the oil for 1 minute without browning it and then stir in the carrot, swede (rutabaga) and potato.

4. Then, sprinkle the cumin and turmeric into the pan and stir in thoroughly.

5. Add the flour and coat the vegetables in it, then gradually add the stock, stirring, bring to the boil, then reduce the heat and simmer for 10-12 minutes.

6. Meanwhile, heat the oven to 400°F/200°C/Gas Mark 6.

7. Finish the pastry by adding just enough cold water to mix it to a soft dough.

8. Roll it out on a lightly floured worktop until it is roughly 1 in (2.5cm) larger all round than your pie dish. Cut a ½ in (12mm) strip from the extra and place it on the lip of the dish.

9. Pour in the filling, then brush the pastry edge with a little water and put the pastry lid on top. Trim the edges, then press to seal and pinch to flute them.

10. Glaze with a little milk or beaten egg, make a hole in the centre and, if liked, garnish with pastry leaves made from the trimmings.

11. Bake in the centre of the oven for 25 minutes until the pastry is golden brown and the filling tender.

SUMMER LASAGNE

Serves 3

Imperial/Metric	USA
6 oz/170g aubergine	6-ounce eggplant
Sea salt	Sea salt
2 tabespoons olive oil	2 tablespoons olive oil
2 oz/55g onion, finely chopped	⅓ cup onion, finely chopped
1 clove garlic, crushed	1 clove garlic, minced
½ stick celery, finely sliced	½ celery stalk, finely sliced
1 teaspoon fresh marjoram, or ½ teaspoon dried	1 teaspoon fresh marjoram, or ½ teaspoon dried
4 oz/115g button mushrooms, wiped and sliced	1½ cups button mushrooms, wiped and sliced
1 lb/455g tomatoes, skinned and chopped	2⅔ cups tomatoes, skinned and chopped
6 sheets wholemeal 'instant' lasagne	6 sheets whole wheat 'instant' lasagne
¾ oz/20g soft vegetable margarine	1½ tablespoons soft vegetable margarine
¾ oz/20g unbleached white flour	Scant ¼ cup unbleached white flour
⅓ pt/200ml skimmed milk	¾ cup skimmed milk
2 oz/55g farmhouse Cheddar, finely grated	½ cup Monterey Jack, finely shredded
1 egg	1 egg
Freshly ground black pepper	Freshly ground black pepper

1. Slice the aubergine (eggplant), sprinkle with sea salt and place a plate on top of the slices. Leave for 30 minutes to draw out the bitterness.

2. Pat dry with kitchen (paper) towel and dice into ½-in (13-mm) cubes.

3. Pour the oil into a saucepan, stir in the aubergine (eggplant), onion and garlic and sauté gently, then stir in the celery, marjoram, mushrooms and tomatoes, bring to the boil, then reduce the heat and simmer for 20 minutes, stirring occasionally.

4. Heat the oven to 375°F/190°C/Gas Mark 5.

5. Place the 'instant' lasagne in a shallow ovenproof dish and pour boiling water over it. Leave it to stand for 5 minutes, then drain just before using.

6. Melt the margarine in a saucepan and stir in the flour.

7. Gradually add the milk, to the margarine and flour, beating well, and slowly bring the sauce to the boil.

8. Reduce the heat slightly and stir in the cheese.

9. Remove from the heat when the cheese has melted and beat in the egg, then season to taste with freshly ground black pepper.

10. Lightly oil a fairly deep ovenproof dish and cover the bottom with 2 lasagne sheets. Then spread half the vegetable mixture over the lasagne, cover this with 2 more lasagne sheets, pour over the rest of the vegetable mixture, cover this with the 2 remaining sheets of lasagne and then pour the cheese sauce over the top.

11. Cover and bake in the centre of the oven for 30 minutes.

MILLET CHEESEBURGERS

Makes 4

These make a tasty light lunch served with a salad. They can be prepared in advance and quickly cooked just before serving.

Imperial/Metric	USA
3 oz/85g millet	Scant ½ cup millet
¾ pt/425ml cold water	2 cups cold water
2 oz/55g onion, finely chopped	⅓ cup onion, finely chopped
4 oz/115g courgette, coarsely grated	1½ cups zucchini, coarsely shredded
2 teaspoons sunflower oil	2 teaspoons safflower oil
1 teaspoon chives, finely chopped	1 teaspoon chives, finely chopped
Sprig fresh tarragon, finely chopped, or ½ teaspoon dried	Sprig fresh tarragon, finely chopped, or ½ teaspoon dried
2 oz/55g farmhouse Cheddar, finely grated	½ cup Monterey Jack, finely grated
Freshly ground black pepper	Freshly ground black pepper
1 tablespoon wholemeal flour	1 tablespoon whole wheat flour
1 egg, beaten	1 egg, beaten
2 oz/55g fresh wholemeal breadcrumbs	1 cup whole wheat bread crumbs
Sunflower oil for frying	Safflower oil for frying

1. Put the millet in a saucepan with the water.
2. Bring to the boil, then cover, reduce the heat and simmer for 20 minutes until the millet is soft and all the liquid has been absorbed.
3. Pour it into a mixing bowl and let it cool.
4. Put the onion and courgette (zucchini) in a pan with the oil and cook gently for 2 minutes.
5. Stir the millet into the onion and courgette (zucchini) mixture, add the herbs and cheese and season to taste with freshly ground black pepper.
6. When thoroughly combined, spread the mixture onto a pie plate and chill for 20 minutes.
7. Cut into quarters and press each quarter into a burger shape, using a

little of the wholemeal (whole wheat) flour if the mixture is a little sticky.

8. Coat each burger first with egg, then with breadcrumbs, shaking off any excess.

9. Chill for 20 minutes.

10. Pour a small amount of sunflower oil in a frying pan (skillet) — just enough to cover the bottom and cook the burgers for 4 minutes each side, or until they are golden brown, then drain off any surplus oil and serve at once.

SLOWLY DOES IT

Slow cooking of stews, casseroles and other savoury dishes needing lengthy cooking times helps to ring the changes in the type of food we eat and, if full use is made of the oven space by baking accompaniments or perhaps a pudding alongside the main course, needn't be wasteful of fuel either.

Warming winter casseroles can be prepared very successfully without meat, using instead lots of colourful beans, lentils, grains and the nutritious root vegetables (parsnips, swede, turnip, carrots and potatoes) while lighter dishes can also be baked slowly.

B OSTON BAKED BEANS

Serves 4

Imperial/Metric	USA
6 oz/170g haricot beans, soaked overnight	⅔ cup navy beans, soaked overnight
1 small onion, finely chopped	1 small onion, finely chopped
½ red pepper, deseeded and finely chopped	½ red sweet pepper, deseeded and finely chopped
1 tablespoon molasses	1 tablespoon molasses
2 tablespoons tomato purée	2 tablespoons tomato paste
½ teaspoon mustard	½ teaspoon mustard
½ teaspoon shoyu sauce	½ teaspoon shoyu sauce
Water	Water

1. Pre-heat the oven to 300°F/150°C/Gas Mark 2.
2. Drain the beans and put them in a flameproof casserole, cover them with cold water and bring to the boil.
3. Add the remaining ingredients, cover, transfer to the oven and bake for 2 hours.
4. Top up with boiling water to the level of the beans and cook for a further 1½ hours.
5. Top up again, if necessary, and cook uncovered for a further 30 minutes until the beans are totally soft. Serve with baked potatoes or chunky wholemeal bread.

LAYERED VEGETABLE BAKE

Serves 4

Imperial/Metric	USA
12 oz/340g frozen spinach, thawed or 1½ lb/680g fresh	1½ cups frozen spinach, or 15 cups fresh
12 oz/340g carrots, scrubbed and finely grated	2 cups carrots, scrubbed and finely grated
1 large onion, sliced into fine rings	1 large onion, sliced into fine rings
8 oz/225g swede, peeled and sliced very finely	1⅓ cups rutabaga, peeled and finely sliced
3 large potatoes, each about 6 oz/170g, peeled and finely sliced	3 large potatoes, each about 6 ounces, peeled and sliced very finely
Freshly ground black pepper	Freshly ground black pepper
½ pt/300ml skimmed milk	1⅓ cups skimmed milk
4 oz/115g farmhouse Cheddar, grated	1 cup Monterey Jack, shredded

1. Pre-heat the oven to 375°F/190°C/Gas Mark 5.

2. Grease a large pie dish or similar ovenproof dish with a knob of butter.

3. If using fresh spinach, wash thoroughly, remove coarse stems and cook until tender, then chop and squeeze out any excess moisture. If using frozen, cook as directed on pack, chop and squeeze out any surplus moisture.

4. Put the spinach in the bottom of the greased dish and cover with the swede (rutabaga) and onion rings, season to taste with freshly ground black pepper, add the carrots, then arrange the potatoes, overlapping the slices, on top.

5. Pour over the milk and sprinkle the cheese on top.

6. Cover and bake for 1-1¼ hours until the vegetables are tender, then cook uncovered for a further 5-10 minutes until the top is golden brown. Serve with crusty bread.

SPICY GOULASH

Serves 2

Imperial/Metric	USA
2 oz/55g onion, finely chopped	⅓ cup onion, finely chopped
4 oz/115g carrot, scrubbed and sliced	⅔ cup carrot, scrubbed and sliced
4 oz/115g parsnip, peeled and chopped into matchsticks	⅔ cup parsnip, peeled and chopped into matchsticks
4 oz/115g borlotti beans, soaked overnight	½ cup pinto beans, soaked overnight
1 oz/30g whole lentils, soaked for 1 hour	2½ tablespoons whole lentils, soaked for 1 hour
¾ pt/425ml water	2 cups water
14 oz/397g tin tomatoes, chopped	14 ounce can tomatoes, chopped
1½ teaspoons paprika	1½ teaspoons paprika
1 bay leaf	1 bay leaf
2 tablespoons sweetcorn	2 tablespoons sweetcorn
Freshly ground black pepper	Freshly ground black pepper

1. Pre-heat the oven to 375°F/190°C/Gas Mark 5.

2. Put the vegetables in an ovenproof dish.

3. Drain the beans and lentils and stir into the vegetables.

4. Stir the water and tomatoes into the vegetables and beans and mix in the paprika, add the bay leaf and sweetcorn and cover.

5. Bake for 1¾-2 hours. Season to taste with freshly ground black pepper, then serve.

CHILLI BEAN BAKE

Serves 4

Imperial/Metric	USA
1 tablespoon sunflower oil	1 tablespoon safflower oil
8 oz/225g onion, finely chopped	1⅓ cups onion, finely chopped
2 sticks celery, chopped	2 celery stalks, chopped
12 oz/340g carrot, scrubbed and diced	2 cups carrot, scrubbed and diced
1 teaspoon ground cumin	1 teaspoon ground cumin
¼ teaspoon cayenne pepper	¼ teaspoon cayenne pepper
4 oz/115g mushrooms, wiped and sliced	1½ cups mushrooms, wiped and sliced
1¼ pt/710ml water	3½ cups water
14 oz/397g tin tomatoes, chopped	14 ounce can tomatoes, chopped
2 dried red chillies	2 dried red chili peppers
4 oz/115g red kidney beans, soaked overnight and drained	½ cup red kidney beans, soaked overnight
4 oz/115g borlotti beans, soaked overnight and drained	½ cup pinto beans soaked overnight
Freshly ground black pepper	Freshly ground black pepper

1. Pre-heat the oven to 375°F/190°C/Gas Mark 5.
2. Pour the oil into a large, flameproof casserole, stir in the onion, celery and carrot and cook for 1 minute.
3. Add the cumin and cayenne pepper and cook for 1 more minute.
4. Stir in the mushrooms, water, tomatoes, chillies (chili peppers) and beans.
5. Bring to the boil, cover, put in the oven and bake for 1¾-2 hours until the beans are tender. Remove the chillies (chili peppers) and season to taste with freshly ground black pepper.

ROOT VEGETABLE COBBLER

Serves 4

A tasty cobbler topping adds extra substance to this warming dish.

Imperial/Metric	USA
1 tablespoon sunflower oil	1 tablespoon safflower oil
1 leek, trimmed and sliced	1 leek, trimmed and sliced
8 oz/225g swede, peeled and diced	1⅓ cups rutabaga, peeled and diced
8 oz/225g parsnip, peeled and diced	1⅓ cups parsnip, peeled and diced
4 oz/115g potato, scrubbed and diced	⅔ cup potato, scrubbed and diced
¾ pt/425ml water	2 cups water
2 tablespoons tomato purée	2 tablespoons tomato paste
½ teaspoon vegetable stock concentrate	½ teaspoon vegetable stock concentrate
½ teaspoon fresh marjoram, chopped, or ¼ teaspoon dried	½ teaspoon fresh marjoram, chopped, or ¼ teaspoon dried
2 teaspoons cornflour mixed with 1 tablespoon cold water	2 teaspoons cornstarch mixed with 1 tablespoon cold water

Topping

6 oz/170g wholemeal flour	1½ cups whole wheat flour
2 teaspoons baking powder	2 teaspoons baking powder
Pinch cayenne pepper	Pinch cayenne pepper
1½ oz/45g soft vegetable margarine	3 tablespoons soft vegetable margarine
3 oz/85g farmhouse Cheddar, grated	¾ cup Monterey Jack, shredded
About ¼ pt/140ml skimmed milk	About ⅔ cup skimmed milk

1. Pour the oil into a saucepan and add the leek, swede (rutabaga), parsnip and potato.
2. Stir together and heat gently for 2 minutes.
3. Add the water, tomato purée (paste), vegetable stock concentrate

and marjoram and bring to the boil, then reduce the heat and simmer for 10 minutes.

4. While the vegetable mixture is cooking, make the topping. Mix together the flour, baking powder and cayenne pepper.

5. Rub (cut) in the margarine.

6. Sprinkle in the cheese and bind to a soft dough with the milk.

7. Heat the oven to 400°F/200°C/Gas Mark 6.

8. Stir the cornflour (cornstarch) into the vegetable mixture and bring to the boil to thicken.

9. Pour into a deep ovenproof dish.

10. Roll out the topping mixture to ½-in (12-mm) thickness.

11. Stamp out 2-in (5-cm) rounds and arrange them in a circle, overlapping, on top of the vegetable mixture.

12. Glaze with a little milk and bake for 20-25 minutes until the topping is well-risen and golden brown.

WINTER BEAN POT

Serves 4

Imperial/Metric	USA
4 oz/115g onion, finely chopped	⅔ cup onion, finely chopped
1 leek, trimmed and sliced	1 leek, trimmed and sliced
1 tablespoon sunflower oil	1 tablespoon safflower oil
8 oz/225g carrot, scrubbed and sliced	1½ cups carrot, scrubbed and sliced
8 oz/225g swede, peeled and diced	1½ cups rutabaga, peeled and diced
14 oz/397g tin tomatoes, chopped	14 ounce can tomatoes, chopped
2¼ pt/1.25 litres water	5⅓ cups water
1 teaspoon vegetable stock concentrate	1 teaspoon vegetable stock concentrate
1 bay leaf	1 bay leaf
2 tablespoons pearl barley	2 tablespoons pot barley
3 oz/85g butter beans, soaked overnight	½ cup lima beans, soaked overnight
3 oz/85g borlotti beans, soaked overnight	Scant ½ cup pinto beans, soaked overnight

1. Place the onion and leek with the oil in a large saucepan and heat gently until softened.

2. Stir in the carrot and swede (rutabaga) and cook for 1 minute.

3. Add the chopped tomatoes, water, stock concentrate, bay leaf, pearl (pot) barley, butter (lima) beans and borlotti (pinto) beans and bring to the boil.

4. Then, either bake in the oven at 375°F/190°C/Gas Mark 5 or cook slowly on the hob for around 1¼-1½ hours until the beans are tender. Serve with chunky bread or baked potatoes.

ACCOMPANIMENTS

When baking the main dish in the oven, maximize fuel by cooking the accompaniment at the same time. For this reason, a range of cooking temperatures rather than a specific temperature is given in each recipe, although, of course, the lower the temperature, the longer it will take to cook, so keep checking it to see if it is done or needs more time. Baked potatoes are obvious choices for casseroles, but here are a few other ideas, too.

OVEN-BAKED RICE

Serves 4

Imperial/Metric	USA
2 teaspoons sunflower oil	2 teaspoons safflower oil
2 oz/55g onion, finely chopped	⅓ cup onion, finely chopped
8 oz/225g long-grain brown rice	1 cup long-grain brown rice
Scant 1 pt/570ml water	Scant 2½ cups water
¼ teaspoon vegetable stock concentrate	¼ teaspoon vegetable stock concentrate

1. Pre-heat the oven to 350-400°F/180-200°C/Gas Mark 4-6.
2. In a flameproof and ovenproof casserole, heat the oil with the onion to soften it gently.
3. Stir in the rice and coat the grains with the oil.
4. Add the water and stock concentrate and bring to the boil.
5. Cover, remove from the heat and put in the oven to bake until tender. Check during cooking just once to ensure that there is sufficient water (all rice varies in the length of cooking time and amount of water required, but it will take a minimum of 20 minutes).

OVEN-BAKED CRACKED WHEAT

Serves 4.

Imperial/Metric	USA
6 oz/170g cracked wheat	**1 cup cracked wheat**
Bay leaf	**Bay leaf**
Freshly ground black pepper	**Freshly ground black pepper**

1. Pre-heat the oven to 350-400°F/180-200°C/gas mark 4-6.

2. Put the cracked wheat in a measuring jug and note the volume it makes.

3. Pour it into an ovenproof dish and add twice its volume of cold water.

4. Add the bay leaf, cover and bake in the oven for 20-30 minutes until the wheat is tender and fluffy.

5. Fork it through, discard the bay leaf and season with freshly ground black pepper.

SPECIAL BAKED POTATOES

Serves 1

Imperial/Metric	USA
1 large baking potato, about 6 oz/170g	1 large baking potato, about 6 ounces
1 oz/30g onion, finely chopped	2 tablespoons onion, finely chopped
1 oz/30g button mushrooms, finely chopped (optional)	½ cup button mushrooms, finely chopped (optional)
Knob unsalted butter, or 2 teaspoons sunflower oil	Knob unsalted butter, or 2 teaspoons safflower oil
Pinch mixed herbs (optional)	Pinch mixed herbs (optional)
Freshly ground black pepper	Freshly ground black pepper
1 oz/30g farmhouse cheese, e.g., Double Gloucester, Cheddar, finely grated	¼ cup hard cheese, e.g., New York Cheddar, finely shredded

1. Pre-heat the oven to 350-400°F/180-200°C/Gas Mark 4-6.
2. Scrub the potato and prick in several places with a fork.
3. Place in the oven for 1-1½ hours or until tender.
4. While the potato is cooking, soften the onion and mushrooms, if using, gently in the butter or oil, then add the herbs, if using.
5. When the potato is cooked, cut it in half lengthwise, but do not cut all the way through. Scoop out the flesh and put it in a mixing bowl.
6. Mash in the onion and mushroom mixture, adding a little skimmed milk if necessary to mash well, and season to taste with freshly ground black pepper.
7. Add half the cheese and beat it in.
8. Pile the potato mixture back into the skin, sprinkling the remaining cheese over.
9. Return to the oven and bake for 10 more minutes.

L AYERED POTATOES

Serves 4

Imperial/Metric	USA
Knob unsalted butter	Knob unsalted butter
1 lb/455g large potatoes, peeled and sliced finely	1 pound large potatoes, peeled and sliced finely
1 small onion, sliced finely into rings	1 small onion, sliced finely into rings
1 clove of garlic (optional)	1 clove of garlic (optional)
Freshly ground black pepper	Freshly ground black pepper
¼ pt/140ml skimmed milk	⅔ cup skimmed milk
2 oz/55g farmhouse Cheddar (optional), finely grated	⅓ cup Monterey Jack (optional), finely shredded

1. Pre-heat the oven to 350-400°F/180-200°C/Gas Mark 4-6.

2. Lightly grease a shallow ovenproof dish with the butter.

3. Arrange half the potato slices in the bottom, overlapping them, add the onion slices and garlic, if using, and season to taste with freshly ground black pepper.

4. Arrange the remaining potato slices on top in the same way and pour over the milk.

5. Season with more pepper, scatter the cheese on top, if using, cover and bake for 1-1½ hours or until tender.

6. Remove the cover and bake for 10 more minutes to make the top crispy.

# RATATOUILLE

Serves 4

A delicious summer 'stew' that has become a classic. Ratatouille is versatile:
it is equally good hot or well-chilled and it can be used as the base of more
sustaining dishes, such as a pie, or topped with cubes of cheese or a savoury
crumble topping (see topping in Nut and Mushroom Bake, page 87).

Imperial/Metric	USA
8 oz/225g aubergine	8-ounce eggplant
Sea salt	Sea salt
2 tablespoons olive oil	2 tablespoons olive oil
4 oz/115g onion, halved then finely sliced	⅔ cup onion, halved then finely sliced
2 cloves garlic, crushed	2 cloves garlic, minced
1 lb/455g tomatoes, skinned and chopped	2⅔ cups tomatoes, skinned and chopped
12 oz/340g courgettes, sliced	Scant 5 cups zucchini, sliced
1 large red pepper, deseeded and cut into 1-in/2.5-cm long strips	1 large red sweet pepper, deseeded and cut into 1-inch long strips
1 large green pepper, deseeded and cut into 1-in/2.5cm long strips	1 large green sweet pepper, deseeded and cut into 1-inch long strips
2 teaspoons fresh basil, or 1 teaspoon dried	2 teaspoons fresh basil, or 1 teaspoon dried
Freshly ground black pepper	Freshly ground black pepper

1. Slice the aubergine (eggplant) into ½-in/13-mm slices.
2. Sprinkle with sea salt, and leave for 30 minutes.
3. Pat dry with kitchen (paper) towel and cut into chunky cubes.
4. Heat the oil in a heavy-based saucepan and add the aubergine
(eggplant) cubes, onion and garlic.
5. Stir well and cook gently for 5 minutes, covered. Stir from time to
time to prevent sticking.
6. Add the tomatoes, courgettes (zucchini), peppers and basil.
7. Cover and simmer for 45 minutes until the vegetables are tender.
Season to taste with freshly ground black pepper and serve.

8 MAKE MEAT GO FURTHER

If the prospect of cutting out meat, fish and fowl, from your diet is just too unappetizing, then make these animal protein foods go further. Instead of serving a fat, quarter-pound steak on *each* plate, make that steak feed two mouths. Extending the animal foods in our diet makes sense on three counts:

- nutritionally — animal foods, especially red meats like beef, lamb and pork, tend to be high in saturated fat;
- environmentally — animal foods — with the exception of fish — take double the resources to produce than vegetable foods as feed has to be produced to nourish the livestock that in turn feed us;
- economically — because animal foods guzzle resources, they are expensive and, ironically, the healthier and leaner, they are, the more costly they are to buy, and, because meat production from animals raised organically is on a small scale, it is, at the moment, most expensive of all.

Consumer demand will encourage farmers to switch to more humane production methods, so help bring about this change by choosing organic or free-range produce wherever possible.

WHAT TO COOK

One of the best ways of making meat go further is to prepare a casserole combining meat with beans and vegetables — it is virtually a meal in one pot. When the casserole is cooking in the oven, try to make the most of the fuel being used by cooking another dish at the same time, for example, jacket potatoes to accompany the casserole, a baked pudding (dessert) or save time as well by making double the quantity of the casserole and freezing half for later — it will only need to be thawed and reheated on the hob. Chicken and fish require less lengthy cooking than beef, lamb or pork joints (cuts) and so are suited to lighter meals that don't need to be cooked in the oven — ideal for summer days when casseroles don't seem so appetizing.

HOW TO COOK

Many casseroles can be prepared on the hob using a good, heavy-based saucepan for cooking, saving fuel by not using the oven. As the heat is more direct, it is important to stir the casserole from time to time to prevent it sticking and to turn the heat down really low so that the pot can just simmer and not boil. A pressure cooker or microwave may also be used for many dishes, which are even more economical uses of energy (see Chapter 3).

L AMB WITH APRICOTS

Serves 4

An unusual combination using dried apricots with pulses (legumes) and meat and the distinctive flavours of coriander and cumin. Rice or cracked wheat (see pages 105 and 106) make good accompaniments and a lightly cooked green vegetable or a green salad would complete the meal.

Imperial/Metric	USA
2 tablespoons olive oil	2 tablespoons olive oil
1 lb/455g lean lamb, boned, trimmed of fat and cut into 1-in/2.5-cm cubes	1 pound lean lamb, boned, trimmed of fat and cut into 1-inch cubes
8 oz/225g onion, halved and finely sliced	1¼ cups onion, halved and finely sliced
2 cloves garlic, crushed	2 cloves garlic, minced
1 teaspoon cumin seeds	1 teaspoon cumin seeds
1 teaspoon coriander seeds	1 teaspoon coriander seeds
1½ pt/850ml lamb, or vegetable stock	3¾ cups lamb, or vegetable stock
6 oz/170g borlotti beans, soaked overnight and drained	¾ cup pinto beans, soaked overnight and drained
4 oz/115g dried apricots	scant cup dried apricots

1. Pre-heat the oven to 325°F/170°C/Gas Mark 3.
2. Heat the oil in a flameproof and ovenproof casserole and brown the lamb cubes on all sides, then remove, draining off the oil into the pot.
3. Stir in the onion, garlic, cumin and coriander seeds and heat together for 1 minute.
4. Stir in the stock, beans and lamb, bring to the boil, cover and cook in the oven for 1 hour.
5. Add the apricots and return to the oven for 45-60 more minutes until the meat and beans are tender. Serve with Oven-baked Rice (see page 105).

SAVOURY MINCE

Serves 4

This tasty way of cooking mince extends the protein by adding plenty of vegetables. Use it as the base for a risotto by stirring in cooked brown rice, for shepherd's pie by topping with mashed potato, as lasagne layered with wholemeal (whole wheat) lasagne and topped with a cheese sauce, or simply serve it with a mound of freshly cooked spaghetti for that ever-popular classic, spaghetti bolognese.

Imperial/Metric	USA
1 tablespoon olive oil	1 tablespoon olive oil
4 oz/115g onion, finely chopped	⅔ cup onion, finely chopped
1 clove garlic, crushed (optional)	1 clove garlic, minced (optional)
½ stick celery, finely chopped	½ celery stalk, finely chopped
8 oz/225g carrot, scrubbed and finely chopped	1⅓ cups carrot, scrubbed and finely chopped
2 teaspoons fresh oregano or marjoram, chopped, or 1 teaspoon dried	2 teaspoons fresh oregano or marjoram, chopped, or 1 teaspoon dried
12 oz/340g lean minced red meat — lamb, pork or beef	12 ounces lean ground round — lamb, pork or beef
1 × 14 oz/397g tin tomatoes	14 ounce can tomatoes
3 tablespoons tomato purée	3 tablespoons tomato paste
1 green or red pepper, deseeded and chopped	1 green or red sweet pepper, deseeded and chopped
4 oz/115g button mushrooms, wiped and sliced	1½ cups button mushrooms, wiped and sliced

1. Put the oil in a large, heavy-based saucepan.
2. Stir in the onion, garlic, if using, celery and carrot and cook gently for 5 minutes without browning.
3. Add the oregano, or marjoram.
4. Break up the mince (ground round) and stir into the pan, browning it all over.
5. Add the tomatoes, breaking them up with the back of your spoon as you mix them in.
6. Stir in the tomato purée (paste), pepper and mushrooms and bring to the boil.
7. Cover, reduce the heat and simmer for 30 minutes. Use as required.

LAMB WITH LEEKS

Serves 4

A complete meal in itself — just serve with chunky, wholemeal bread.

Imperial/Metric	USA
4 lamb chump chops or 8 small cutlets	4 lamb rib chops or 8 breast riblets
2 tablespoons olive oil	2 tablespoons olive oil
2 leeks, trimmed and cut into ½-in/13-mm slices	2 leeks, trimmed and cut into ½-inch slices
8 oz/225g carrot, scrubbed and sliced	1⅓ cups carrot, scrubbed and sliced
2 sticks celery, cut into ½-in/13-mm slices	2 celery stalks, cut into ½-inch slices
4 oz/115g butter beans, soaked overnight and drained	⅔ cup lima beans, soaked overnight and drained
Sprig fresh rosemary, or ½ teaspoon dried	Sprig fresh rosemary, or ½ teaspoon dried
1¾ pt/1 litre water	4½ cups water
½ teaspoon vegetable stock concentrate	½ teaspoon vegetable stock concentrate
1 tablespoon cornflour, mixed with 2 tablespoons cold water	1 tablespoon cornstarch, mixed with 2 tablespoons cold water
Freshly ground black pepper	Freshly ground black pepper

1. Pre-heat the oven to 325°F/170°C/Gas Mark 3.
2. Wash the lamb and pat dry with kitchen (paper) towel and remove any excess fat.
3. Heat the oil in a flameproof and ovenproof casserole and add the chops, or cutlets (riblets).
4. Brown on both sides and then remove from the heat, draining off the oil into the pan.
5. Stir in the leeks, carrots and celery and cook for 1 minute.
6. Add the beans, rosemary, water, vegetable stock concentrate and lamb, bring to the boil, then cover and cook in the oven for 1½ hours until the lamb and beans are tender.
7. Stir in the cornflour (cornstarch) and water mixture and return to the oven for 5 minutes to thicken the gravy.

8. Season to taste with freshly ground black pepper and serve.

SUMMER KEBABS

Serves 4

Imperial/Metric	USA
1¼ lb/565g chicken breasts, boned, wiped and cut into 1-in/2.5-cm cubes	1¼ pounds chicken breasts, boned, wiped and cut into 1-inch cubes
Juice of ½ lemon	Juice ½ lemon
2 tablespoons olive oil	2 tablespoons olive oil
1 teaspoon fresh tarragon, chopped, or ½ teaspoon dried	1 teaspoon fresh tarragon, chopped, or ½ teaspoon dried
Freshly ground black pepper	Freshly ground black pepper
4 small courgettes, cut into ½-in/13-mm slices	4 small zucchini, cut into ½-inch slices
12 button mushrooms, wiped	12 button mushrooms, wiped
4 small onions, peeled and quartered	4 small onions, peeled and quartered
1 red pepper, deseeded and cut into 1-in/2.5-cm squares	1 red sweet pepper, deseeded and cut into 1-inch squares

1. Put the chicken cubes into a bowl.
2. Shake the lemon juice and olive oil together with the tarragon and some freshly ground black pepper in a screw-top jar, then pour the mixture over the chicken and mix it in well.
3. Cover and leave to marinate in the fridge for at least 1 hour.
4. Meanwhile, prepare the barbecue or heat the grill (broiler) a few minutes before you are ready to cook and have ready 4 large barbecue skewers or 8 small skewers.
5. When ready to cook, divide the chicken into 4 piles, then thread it and the vegetables alternately onto the skewers.
6. Baste the kebabs with the marinade and cook for 12-15 minutes, turning and basting them until the chicken is cooked through. Serve with a salad and rice.

CHICKEN AND POTATO BAKE

Serves 4

Imperial/Metric	USA
2 oz/55g unsalted butter	¼ cup unsalted butter
12-14 oz/340-395g chicken breast fillets, wiped and cut into ½ x 1-in/13-mm x 25-mm strips	12-14 ounces chicken breast fillets, wiped and cut into ½ x 1-inch strips
8 oz/225g onion, finely sliced	1⅓ cups onion, finely sliced
2 teaspoons fresh tarragon, chopped, or 1 teaspoon dried	2 teaspoons fresh tarragon, chopped, or 1 teaspoon dried
1 clove garlic, crushed (optional)	1 clove garlic, minced (optional)
1¼ lb/565g large potatoes, peeled and finely sliced	3½ cups large potatoes, peeled and finely sliced
¼ pt/140ml single cream	⅔ cup light cream
About ¼ pt/140ml skimmed milk, or single cream	About ⅔ cup skimmed milk, or light cream
Freshly ground black pepper	Freshly ground black pepper

1. Pre-heat the oven to 375°F/190°C/Gas Mark 5.

2. Melt the butter in a frying pan (skillet) over a low heat and stir in the chicken.

3. Cook it quickly on all sides until it turns white, then remove from the pan using a fish slice (slotted spoon) to drain off the butter.

4. Stir in the onion, tarragon and garlic, if using and fry until the onions begin to turn golden, then remove them from pan.

5. Lightly grease an ovenproof casserole using the fat remaining in the pan.

6. Arrange a layer of half the potato slices in the bottom of the casserole, overlapping them as you do so.

7. Pour in the chicken and onion mixture and arrange the remaining potato slices, overlapping on top.

8. Beat together the cream and milk, or just cream, seasoning with freshly ground black pepper, and pour over the potatoes, adding enough extra milk to bring the level to just below the top layer of potatoes.

9. Cover and bake for about 1-1¼ hours, until the chicken and potato are tender, then remove the cover and brown for 10 minutes (test with the blade of a knife from time to time: if the potatoes take more than

1 hour to soften, check that there is enough liquid). Serve with lightly cooked broccoli.

SMOKED MACKEREL RISOTTO

Serves 4

Smoked mackerel is usually served just as it is with a salad, but the fish is so tasty that it can also be used to brighten up rice. This dish is equally good cold.

Imperial/Metric	USA
1 tablespoon sunflower oil, or ¾ oz/20g unsalted butter	1 tablespoon safflower oil, or scant 2 tablespoons unsalted butter
2 sticks celery, finely sliced	2 celery stalks, finely sliced
4 oz/115g onion, finely chopped	⅔ cup onion, finely chopped
10 oz/285g long-grain brown rice	1¼ cups long-grain brown rice
1½ pt/850ml water	3¾ cups water
8 oz/225g fresh French beans, cut into 1-in/2.5-cm lengths	½ cup fresh string beans, cut into 1-inch lengths
8 oz/225g sweetcorn	1⅓ cups sweetcorn
½ teaspoon dried mixed herbs	½ teaspoon dried mixed herbs
12 oz/340g smoked mackerel fillets	12 ounces smoked mackerel fillets

1. Heat the oil, or butter, in a saucepan and stir in the celery and onion.
2. Cook them gently without browning for 2 minutes.
3. Stir in the rice, coating the grains with the oil, or butter.
4. Add the water and bring to the boil.
5. Stir in the beans, sweetcorn and herbs and reduce the heat.
6. Cover and simmer for 15-20 minutes, or until the rice is tender and the water has been absorbed.
7. While the rice is cooking, remove the skin from the smoked mackerel, discard any bones and flake the meat.
8. When the rice is ready, stir the mackerel into it and serve at once.

BRAISED LIVER WITH VEGETABLES

Serves 4

Liver is a storehouse of iron and vitamin A, but it is not to everyone's liking. Casseroling rather than frying it makes a more acceptable dish and the addition of vegetables makes it even more nourishing, so if you don't eat liver as a rule, try this and be pleasantly surprised.

Imperial/Metric	USA
1 lb/455g lambs' liver, washed, trimmed and cut into 2-in/5-cm strips	1 pound lambs' liver, washed, trimmed and cut into 2-inch strips
1 oz/30g wholemeal flour	¼ cup whole wheat flour
4 oz/115g onion, finely sliced	⅔ cup onion, finely sliced
6 oz/170g carrot, scrubbed and sliced	1⅓ cups carrot, scrubbed and sliced
6 oz/170g swede, peeled and diced	1⅓ cups rutabaga, peeled and diced
2 sticks celery, sliced	2 celery stalks, sliced
1 small dessert apple, peeled, cored and diced	1 small sweet apple, peeled, cored and diced
1 teaspoon fresh sage, chopped, or ½ teaspoon dried	1 teaspoon fresh sage, chopped, or ½ teaspoon dried
1½ pt/850ml water	3¾ cups water
½ teaspoon vegetable stock concentrate	½ teaspoon vegetable stock concentrate
Freshly ground black pepper	Freshly ground black pepper

1. Pre-heat the oven to 350°F/180°C/Gas Mark 4.
2. Toss the liver strips in the flour, then put them in the bottom of an ovenproof casserole dish.
3. Add the onion, carrot, swede (rutabaga), celery and apple and mix together well.
4. Add the sage, water and vegetable stock concentrate, cover and bake in the oven for 1½ hours.
5. Season to taste with freshly ground black pepper and serve with baked potatoes.

PORK AND VEGETABLE BRAISE

Serves 4

Choose the leanest pork chops you can find for this colourful dish. Pork steaks without the bone could also be used.

Imperial/Metric	USA
4 rindless pork chops, each about 6 oz/170g	4 rindless pork chops, each about 6 ounces
2 leeks, trimmed and cut into ½-in/13-mm rings	2 leeks, trimmed and cut into ½-inch rings
1 lb/455g swede, peeled and cut into ½-in/13-mm cubes	2⅔ cups rutabaga, peeled and cut into ½-inch cubes
8 oz/225g carrot, scrubbed and sliced	1⅓ cups carrot, scrubbed and sliced
1 stick celery, sliced	1 celery stalk, sliced
2×14 oz/397g tin tomatoes, roughly chopped	2×14 ounce can tomatoes, roughly chopped
3 oz/85g butter beans, soaked overnight and drained	½ cup lima beans, soaked overnight and drained
1 bay leaf	1 bay leaf
½ pt/285ml water	1⅓ cups water
¾ teaspoon vegetable stock concentrate	¾ teaspoon vegetable stock concentrate
2 fresh sage leaves, chopped, or ½ teaspoon dried	2 fresh sage leaves, chopped, or ½ teaspoon dried

1. Pre-heat the oven to 350°F/180°C/Gas Mark 4.
2. Wash the pork chops and pat them dry with kitchen (paper) towel and put them in the bottom of a large ovenproof casserole.
3. Add the leeks, swede (rutabaga), carrots, and celery.
4. Add the tomatoes and the butter (lima) beans, bay leaf, water, stock concentrate and sage and stir together thoroughly.
5. Cover and bake for 1½-2 hours until the beans and swede (rutabaga) are just tender. Serve with baked potatoes.

FAMILY FISH PIE

Serves 4

An old favourite that makes fish go a long way and is warming and nourishing on a cold winter's evening. Vary the fish by using smoked cod or haddock (coloured with a natural dye or, preferably, uncoloured).

Imperial/Metric	USA
1¼ lb/565g cod, haddock or coley fillet	1¼ pound cod, Finnan haddock or coley fillet
½ pt/285ml cold water	1⅓ cups cold water
1½ lb/680g potatoes, peeled and cut into 2-in/5-cm pieces	3 cups potatoes, peeled and cut into 2-inch pieces
1½ oz/45g unsalted butter, or vegetable margarine	3 tablespoons unsalted butter, or vegetable margarine
4 oz/115g onion, finely chopped	⅔ cup onion, finely chopped
1½ oz/45g unbleached white flour	Heaped ¼ cup unbleached white flour
½ pt/285ml skimmed milk	1⅓ cups skimmed milk
Freshly ground black pepper	Freshly ground black pepper
4 eggs, hard-boiled, chopped	4 eggs, hard-cooked, chopped
Knob unsalted butter	Knob unsalted butter
Skimmed milk, to mash	Skimmed milk, to mash
1 oz/30g farmhouse Cheddar, finely grated	¼ cup Monterey Jack, finely shredded

1. Put the fish in a shallow poaching pan with the water, bring slowly to the boil, then reduce the heat and poach gently until the fish is just cooked.

2. Strain off the liquid and reserve it for making the sauce.

3. Put the potatoes in a pan of cold water, bring to the boil and cook until soft.

4. Melt the butter, or margarine, in a pan and stir in the onion, then cover and allow to sweat gently until the onion is soft.

5. Stir in the flour, mixing thoroughly, and gradually add the milk and enough poaching liquid to make a smooth, fairly thick sauce.

6. Season to taste with freshly ground black pepper.

7. Remove the sauce from the heat and stir in the egg.

8. Flake the fish, removing any skin and bones, and stir it into the sauce.

9. Drain and mash the potatoes with the knob of butter and sufficient milk and season to taste with freshly ground black pepper.

10. Heat the grill (broiler) and pour the sauce into a warmed serving dish, top it with the potato and sprinkle the cheese over.

11. Put the pie under the grill (broiler) to brown. Serve with a lightly cooked green vegetable.

CHICKEN WITH CIDER AND TOMATOES

Serves 4

Imperial/Metric	USA
1 tablespoon olive oil	1 tablespoon olive oil
4 part-boned chicken breasts, skinned and wiped	4 part-boned chicken breasts, skinned and wiped
4 oz/115g onion, finely sliced	⅔ cup onion, finely sliced
1 red, or green, pepper, deseeded and sliced	1 red, or green, sweet pepper, deseeded and sliced
8 oz/225g courgettes, sliced	Scant cup zucchini, sliced
2×14 oz/397g tin tomatoes, chopped	2×14 ounce can tomatoes, chopped
½ pt/285ml dry cider	1⅛ cups cider
2 teaspoons fresh marjoram, chopped, or 1 teaspoon dried	2 teaspoons fresh marjoram, chopped, or 1 teaspoon dried
1 bay leaf	1 bay leaf
Freshly ground black pepper	Freshly ground black pepper

1. Pre-heat the oven to 350°F/180°C/Gas Mark 4.

2. Heat the oil in a flameproof and ovenproof casserole and quickly sear the chicken breasts on each side, then remove them from the casserole.

3. Stir in the onion and heat it for 1 minute.

4. Now add the (sweet) pepper, courgettes (zucchini) and tomatoes.

5. Return the chicken breasts to the pot, pour over the cider and sprinkle in the marjoram and bay leaf.

6. Put the casserole in the oven and bake for 1½-1¾ hours until the chicken is tender.

7. Season with freshly ground black pepper and serve with baked potatoes or *al dente* pasta shells.

BAKED COD CRUMBLE

Serves 4

Imperial/Metric	USA
Crumble topping	
2 oz/55g wholemeal flour	½ cup whole wheat flour
2 oz/55g rolled oats	½ cup rolled oats
1 tablespoon sesame seeds	1 tablespoon sesame seeds
2 oz/55g soft vegetable margarine	¼ cup soft vegetable margarine
Pinch mustard powder	Pinch mustard powder
Pinch cayenne pepper	Pinch cayenne pepper
Freshly ground black pepper	Freshly ground black pepper

Filling	
4 oz/115g onion, finely chopped	⅔ cup onion, finely chopped
2 teaspoons olive oil	2 teaspoons olive oil
14 oz/397g tin tomatoes, chopped	14 ounce can tomatoes, chopped
1 lb/455g cod fillet, skinned and cut into 1-in/2.5-cm cubes	1-pound cod fillet, skinned and cut into 1-inch cubes
4 oz/115g button mushrooms, wiped and sliced	1½ cups button mushrooms, wiped and sliced
1 teaspoon fresh basil, chopped, or ½ teaspoon dried	1 teaspoon fresh basil, chopped, or ½ teaspoon dried

1. Pre-heat the oven to 400°F/200°C/Gas Mark 6.
2. Put the flour, oats and seeds in a mixing bowl and rub (cut) in the margarine.
3. Stir in the spices and season with freshly ground black pepper.

1. Put the onion in a pan with the olive oil and cook for 1 minute.
2. Stir in the tomatoes, bring to the boil, then remove from the heat and stir in the cod cubes, mushrooms and basil.
3. Pour the fish, onion and mushroom mixture into an ovenproof dish, sprinkle the crumble topping on top and bake in the oven for 15-20 minutes until the topping is golden brown.

9 BAKING AT HOME

Home baking has gone out of fashion as in-store bakeries and countless ready-made foods have arrived, but baking at home has much to commend it. It's cheap, it maximizes usage of fuel, it can be healthy and, surprisingly, it doesn't take too much time either.

THE COST

Good-quality 'real' bread, made from organic flour, costs you more in the shops than mass-produced white sliced. You pay for the extra costs involved in getting that small-scale speciality loaf to the shop shelf. In much the same way, organic wholemeal (whole wheat) flour costs more than standard plain white flour, but, even so, baking with top-quality ingredients at home will *still* be cheaper than buying ready-baked bread of the same quality — *and* you can prepare it with just the combination of ingredients you want. If you want to look after your health and cut down on the salt in your diet you can reduce the level of salt in a recipe; if you want to avoid all sugar, you can leave out the sugar (it's only added to speed up the action of the yeast initially anyway) and there'll be no artificial additives such as dough improvers, preservatives and other ingredients deemed necessary by food manufacturers. With practice, the last thing you'll have to worry about is the keeping quality of home-made bread — there simply won't be the need!

THE FUEL

Making optimum use of the oven when it is being used to prepare a meal makes economic as well as ecological sense. Baked goods, such as a tart or crumble for a dessert, or cakes or biscuits (cookies), can be baked alongside another dish requiring roughly the same oven temperature. Cakes and biscuits (cookies) need more careful cooking so, when doubling up on oven space, their cooking temperature should take priority (a casserole, for example, is not affected by being cooked at a temperature slightly higher or lower).

Bread is the exception as few foods require such a fierce oven as bread. The high temperature is essential for stopping the reaction of the yeast before it over proves (rises) and ruins the dough. Few foods can therefore be cooked at the same time as bread, but make the best use of the fuel by baking a batch of bread rather than just one loaf. Similarly, pastry cases (pie crusts) can be prepared in batches, too. Several quiche cases (crusts), for example, can be baked without fillings when a pie or tart is being made and then frozen for later use.

THE NUTRITIONAL VALUE

Baked goods can be sweet or savoury or, like bread, they can bridge the gap. It is desirable to cut down on sweet things but, for treats, it is healthier to choose cakes and biscuits (cookies) made from wholemeal (whole wheat) flour, honey, dried fruits and soft vegetable margarine rather than the highly sweetened and fatty sticky buns and cream cakes that you see in most baker's windows. It's all a question of moderation, of course!

All the recipes in this section use wholemeal (whole wheat) flour as it contains double the fibre of white flour, vitamin B_6, folic acid, biotin and nicotinic acid (all B vitamins), four times the level of vitamin B_2 and more B_1, zinc, iron and magnesium than white. If that weren't enough, it has a delicious nutty flavour, too!

BASIC WHOLEMEAL BREAD

Makes 2×1 lb/455g loaves

Imperial/Metric	USA
1½ lb/680g wholemeal flour	4 cups whole wheat flour
½-1 teaspoon sea salt	½-1 teaspoon sea salt
1 oz/30g soft vegetable margarine	2 tablespoons butter
1 oz/30g fresh yeast	2½ tablespoons fresh yeast
¾ pt/425ml tepid water	2 cups lukewarm water
1×25mg vitamin C tablet, crushed	1×25mg vitamin C tablet, crushed
1 teaspoon clear honey (optional)	1 teaspoon clear honey (optional)
1 egg beaten, or skimmed milk to glaze	1 egg beaten, or skimmed milk to glaze
Sesame seeds, sunflower seeds, oatmeal or poppy seeds to garnish if liked	Sesame seeds, sunflower seeds, oatmeal or poppy seeds to garnish if liked

1. Mix the flour with the salt and rub (cut) in the margarine thoroughly.

2. Crumble the yeast into the water, add the vitamin C tablet and stir in well until the yeast has dissolved.

3. Pour the yeast mixture on to the flour and margarine mixture and mix together using your hands, drawing the dough together (different flours absorb different amounts of water so you may find that you need slightly more liquid to obtain a smooth dough, but equally you may need to add an extra sprinkling of flour).

4. Turn the dough out onto a lightly floured work surface and knead it well. (Kneading helps to distribute the yeast uniformly throughout the dough and to ensure that the bread will rise evenly develops the gluten from the flour and this helps the bread to rise well. Kneading can be done quite energetically using both hands. Fold the ball of dough towards you and then push down and away with the palm of your hand. Give it a quarter turn and repeat, developing a rocking rhythm. You may find that the dough becomes sticky as you work it — just add a little extra flour as required.) Knead for about 10 minutes — until the dough feels firm, smooth and elastic — then cover it with the mixing bowl, upturned, or a cloth and let it rest (stand) for 10 minutes.

5. Meanwhile, lightly grease 2 × 1 lb/455g loaf tins (pans) or two baking sheets and pre-heat the oven to 450°F/230°C/Gas Mark 8.

6. Divide the dough into two equal halves, then, if making loaves, gently pull each half into a rectangle 3 times the width of the tin (pan). Fold it in three into itself and place it in the prepared tin (pan) with the edge underneath or shape into round or sausage shapes and place on the baking sheets. (If making rolls, shape as desired and arrange, spaced apart, on the prepared baking sheets.)

7. Place the tins (pans) or sheets in a warm place and cover with a slightly damp tea-towel (dish towel) or with lightly greased polythene, then leave to prove (rise) until they have almost doubled in size — they are ready when they spring back when lightly pressed with a fingertip (don't over-prove (rise) or the dough will loose its elasticity and collapse).

8. Glaze the bread with either egg or milk and sprinkle over your chosen topping(s) — or simply glaze.

9. Bake at the top of the oven for 30-40 minutes for loaves, or 15-20 minutes for rolls. The bread is ready when it is golden brown and sounds hollow when tapped on the bottom.

10. Remove the loaves from the tins (pans), or the rolls from the baking sheets, and let cool on cooling racks.

S HAPES OF BREAD

Attractive loaves and rolls can be baked by shaping the dough in a variety of ways. Here are a few which can be made using half the Basic Wholemeal Bread dough (see page 124) to make either one special loaf or a batch of 20 rolls that are miniature versions of it.

TRADITIONAL BRITISH COTTAGE LOAF

Divide the dough into 2 pieces, 1 twice as big as the other. Shape each into a round and put the largest underneath on the baking sheet. Place the smaller one on top and, using a fingertip, which has been dipped in flour, press firmly through the centre to make an indentation.

CROWN

Divide the dough into 7 equal pieces. Shape each into a round and place them inside a lightly greased deep 7-in/18-cm round cake tin (pan), with one in the centre (only suitable for loaves).

PLAIT (BRAID)

Divide the dough into three equal portions. Roll each into a sausage shape about 12-in/30-cm long (or 4-in/10-cm long if making individual rolls). Lay them side by side on the work surface, pinch the ends together and plait (braid) loosely. Tuck in the bottom ends and transfer to the baking sheet.

VIENNA

Shape the dough into a round and leave it to prove (rise). When it is ready, cut diagonal slashes across the top and bake.

COBURG

Shape the dough into a round and leave it to prove (rise). When it is ready, slash a cross into the top of the dough.

ROLLS

As well as the above, rolls can be shaped as follows.

SPIRALS
Roll each portion of dough into a long sausage shape, then roll them up to form spirals or the letter 'S'.

KNOTS
Roll each portion of dough into a long sausage shape and tie loosely into a knot.

BATCH BAKING BREAD

Bread dough can be prepared in larger amounts simply by doubling up the quantities. Bread freezes well, so baking a large batch in one go makes the most of the time and energy — yours and the oven's. The dough can also be frozen uncooked. When you need it, simply thaw it out, leave it to prove (rise) and then bake it as normal. It is useful to pack the dough for the freezer in small amounts — enough for one loaf or a smaller amount, say for 5 rolls.

Bread dough can also be used as a base for savoury dishes. Pizza Pie (see page 130), a deep pan pizza, is one, or rolling up the dough with a savoury filling spread on it is a delicious other.

QUICK SODA BREAD

Makes 1 large loaf

Soda bread takes only 25 minutes to cook and little time to prepare so is an unusual and time-saving change from conventional yeast-baked bread. It's also invaluable for those on a yeast-free diet.

Imperial/Metric	USA
1 lb/455g wholemeal flour	4 cups whole wheat flour
2½ teaspoons baking powder	2½ teaspoons baking powder
½ teaspoon sea salt	½ teaspoon sea salt
½ pt/285ml buttermilk	1⅓ cups buttermilk
¼ pt/140ml skimmed milk	⅔ cup skimmed milk

1. Heat the oven to 450°F/230°C/Gas Mark 7.

2. Lightly grease a baking sheet.

3. Sieve (sift) the flour, baking powder and salt together into a large mixing bowl and add the bran left in the sieve (strainer).

4. Stir in the buttermilk using the blade of a knife and add just enough skimmed milk to mix to a soft dough.

5. Turn it out onto a floured surface and knead the dough gently, forming it into an 8-in/20-cm round.

6. Put it on the baking sheet and cut a large cross through the centre, from top to bottom and side to side.

7. Glaze the loaf with a little skimmed milk and bake in the centre of the oven for 25-30 minutes, until it is well risen and golden brown. Serve hot, breaking the bread into the 4 equal segments made by the cross.

WHOLEMEAL PASTRY

Makes 4 oz/115g, sufficient to line a 7-in/18-cm quiche or small pie dish.

Imperial/Metric	USA
4 oz/115g wholemeal flour	**1 cup whole wheat flour**
Pinch sea salt (optional)	**Pinch sea salt (optional)**
2 oz/55g soft vegetable margarine	**¼ cup soft vegetable margarine**
Cold water to mix	**Cold water to mix**

1. Sift the flour into a mixing bowl with the salt, if using, and add the bran remaining in the sieve (strainer).

2. Chop the margarine into small pieces and rub (cut) into the flour using your fingertips until the mixture resembles fine breadcrumbs. (At this stage it is useful to chill the mixture for 15 minutes as this makes the pastry easier to handle.)

3. Add just enough cold water to mix to a soft dough.

4. Gently knead it with your fingertips and then turn it out on to a lightly floured surface and roll out as required.

Variations: *Sesame pastry*: add 1 tablespoon sesame seeds to the flour.

Oat pastry: substitute ½ oz/15g/2 tablespoons rolled oats for ½ oz/15g/2 tablespoons of the flour.

Cheese pastry: add 2 oz/55g/½ cup finely grated (shredded) farmhouse Cheddar (Monterey Jack) and a pinch each of mustard powder and cayenne pepper to the flour once the margarine has been rubbed (cut) in.

Sweet pastry: no need to add sugar; simply add the yolk of an egg to the flour in place of some of the water.

PIZZA PIE

Serves 4

Imperial/Metric	USA
8 oz/225g of Basic Wholemeal Bread dough (see page 124)	8 ounces of Whole Wheat Bread dough (see page 124)
1 clove garlic, crushed	1 clove garlic, minced
2 oz/55g onion, finely chopped	⅓ cup onion, finely chopped
1 tablespoon olive oil	1 tablespoon olive oil
2 teaspoons fresh oregano, chopped, or 1 teaspoon dried	2 teaspoons fresh oregano, chopped, or 1 teaspoon dried
1 small red pepper, deseeded and finely chopped	1 small red sweet pepper, deseeded and finely chopped
14 oz/397g tin tomatoes, chopped	14 ounce can tomatoes, chopped
6 oz/170g button mushrooms, wiped and finely chopped	2¼ cups button mushrooms, wiped and finely chopped
1 small green pepper, deseeded and finely chopped	1 small green sweet pepper, deseeded and finely chopped
8 oz/225g Mozzarella cheese, very finely sliced	2⅔ cup Mozzarella cheese, very finely sliced

1. Make the dough as given on page 124.

2. After kneading, put it wrapped, in the fridge while you prepare the pizza sauce.

3. Put the garlic and onion in a saucepan with the olive oil and cook gently.

4. Stir in half the oregano and all the red (sweet) pepper and the tomatoes, bring to the boil, then simmer for 20 minutes until the sauce is thick and pulpy.

5. Heat the oven to 450°F/230°C/Gas Mark 8.

6. Lightly oil an ovenproof pizza plate or baking sheet.

7. Shape the dough into a 10-in/25.5-cm round, or to fit the size of the pizza plate, and press the centre down a little to form a 'pie crust' round the edge.

8. Pour the sauce on top of the dough and arrange the mushrooms and green (sweet) pepper on top and the Mozzarella on top of that.

9. Put the pizza at the top of the oven (the oven must have reached the temperature for best results) and bake until the cheese has melted, is bubbling and turning golden brown. Serve at once, cut into 4 large wedges.

PICNIC PASTIES

Makes 4

Cheap and easy to make, these are ideal for packed lunches.

Imperial/Metric	USA
Double quantity of Wholemeal Pastry (see page 129)	Double quantity of Whole Wheat Pastry (see page 129)
2 oz/55g onion, finely chopped	⅓ cup onion, finely chopped
4 oz/115g carrot, scrubbed and finely diced	⅔ cup carrot, scrubbed and finely diced
4 oz/115g potato, scrubbed and finely diced	⅔ cup potato, scrubbed and finely diced
2 oz/55g sweetcorn	4 tablespoons sweetcorn
1 tablespoon water	1 tablespoon water
2 oz/55g farmhouse Cheddar, finely grated	½ cup Monterey Jack, finely shredded
¼ teaspoon dried mixed herbs	¼ teaspoon dried mixed herbs
Skimmed milk to glaze	Skimmed milk to glaze
Sesame seeds to garnish	Sesame seeds to garnish

1. Pre-heat the oven to 400°F/200°C/Gas Mark 6.
2. Divide the pastry into four and roll each out to a 6-in/15-cm round, using a side plate as a guide, and cut out.
3. Mix together the onion, carrot, potato, sweetcorn, water, cheese and herbs.
4. Divide the vegetable mixture between the 4 pastry circles, forming it into a line down the centre of each circle.
5. Brush the edges of each circle with cold water and lift the edges up and together to meet over the filling.
6. Seal them by pressing together and flute the seam with the aid of the back of a knife.
7. Place the pasties on a greased baking sheet and glaze them with skimmed milk.
8. Sprinkle the sesame seeds on top of each pasty and bake in the centre of the oven for 25 minutes until the filling is soft and the tops are golden brown. Serve either warm or cold.

LEEK AND ALMOND QUICHE

Serves 4

Imperial/Metric	USA
6 oz/170g of Wholemeal Pastry (see page 129), made with 6 oz/170g wholemeal flour and 3 oz/85g soft vegetable margarine	6 ounces of Whole Wheat Pastry (see page 129), made with 6 ounces whole wheat flour and 3 ounces soft vegetable margarine
1 lb/455g leeks, trimmed and cut into ½-in/13-mm slices	4 cups leeks, trimmed and cut into ½-inch slices
3 eggs	3 eggs
½ teaspoon fresh rosemary, or ¼ teaspoon dried	½ teaspoon fresh rosemary, or ¼ teaspoon dried
Freshly ground black pepper	Freshly ground black pepper
1 oz/30g flaked almonds	¼ cup slivered almonds
2 oz/55g Stilton, or strong farmhouse Cheddar, finely grated	½ cup Stilton, or other blue cheese, or New York Cheddar, finely shredded

1. Pre-heat the oven to 400°F/200°C/Gas Mark 6.

2. Make the pastry, line an 8-in/20-cm round flan dish (tart pan), cut out an 8-in/20-cm diameter of greaseproof (waxed) paper, put it in the bottom of the pastry case (pie crust), fill with dried beans and bake for 10 minutes.

3. Pour a small amount of water into a pan, bring to the boil and add the leeks.

4. Cook for 5 minutes until just tender, then drain, reserving the water.

5. When the pastry is cooked, arrange the leek slices in the bottom.

6. Beat the eggs in a measuring jug with the rosemary and season with freshly ground black pepper, then make the quantity up to ½ pt/285ml/2 cups with the reserved cooking water from the leeks and beat together well.

7. Pour the egg mixture over the leeks.

8. Scatter the almonds and cheese on top and bake in the centre of the oven for 25-30 minutes until the topping is golden brown and the filling has set. Serve hot or cold.

CHEESY FLAPJACKS

Makes 10 Flapjacks

Imperial/Metric	USA
5 oz/140g rolled oats	1¼ cups rolled oats
1 oz/30g sunflower seeds	2 tablespoons sunflower seeds
1 oz/30g sesame seeds	2 tablespoons sesame seeds
¼ teaspoon mustard powder	¼ teaspoon mustard powder
3 oz/85g farmhouse Cheddar, finely grated	¾ cup Monterey Jack, finely shredded
1 egg	1 egg
2 tablespoons skimmed milk	2 tablespoons skimmed milk
3 oz/85g soft vegetable margarine	⅓ cup soft vegetable margarine

1. Pre-heat the oven to 350°F/180°C/Gas Mark 4.

2. Lightly oil a shallow 8-in/20-cm square tin (pan).

3. Combine the oats, sunflower and sesame seeds and mustard with the cheese in a mixing bowl.

4. Beat the egg with the milk.

5. Melt the margarine and pour it on to the dry ingredients, mixing in the egg and milk mixture at the same time.

6. Stir everything together until it is well combined and then, spread it in the prepared tin (pan), smoothing the top.

7. Bake the flapjacks in the centre of the oven for 25-30 minutes, or until the top is well browned.

8. Mark into 10 fingers while still hot, then leave to cool in the tin (pan) before carefully removing them.

BAKEWELL TART

Serves 4

A wholemeal (whole wheat) version of this traditional British family favourite. It always goes down well!

Imperial/Metric	USA
4 oz/115g Wholemeal Pastry (see page 129)	4 ounces Whole Wheat Pastry (see page 129)
2 oz/55g soft vegetable margarine	¼ cup soft vegetable margarine
2 oz/55g muscovado sugar	⅓ cup soft dark brown sugar
1 egg	1 egg
1½ oz/45g ground almonds	⅓ cup ground almonds
2½ oz/70g wholemeal flour	Heaped ½ cup whole wheat flour
1 teaspoon baking powder	1 teaspoon baking powder
1 tablespoon skimmed milk	1 tablespoon skimmed milk
3 tablespoons no-added sugar raspberry jam	3 tablespoons no-added sugar raspberry jelly
1 oz/30g flaked almonds	¼ cup slivered almonds

1. Pre-heat the oven to 375°F/190°C/Gas Mark 5.
2. Roll out the pastry to fit a greased fluted 7-in/18-cm loose-bottomed flan tin or dish (tart pan) and line with pastry.
3. Beat the margarine and sugar together until light and fluffy, then beat in the egg.
4. Sieve (sift) together the almonds, flour and baking powder, then gently fold the dry mixture into the margarine, sugar and egg mixture.
5. Mix in just enough skimmed milk to give a light dropping consistency.
6. Spread the jam in the bottom of the pastry case (pie crust), then spoon the almond mixture on top and level.
7. Gather the pastry trimmings together, roll out and cut into fine strips long enough to lay across the tart in a lattice pattern.
8. Sprinkle the almonds in the spaces.
9. Glaze the pastry lightly with skimmed milk, then bake the tart in the centre of the oven for 20-25 minutes until the almond mixture springs back when lightly pressed with a fingertip. Serve hot or cold.

CARROT CAKE

Makes 1 deep, 7-in/18-cm-round cake

A deliciously light cake that keeps well for a couple of days — if there's any left!

Imperial/Metric	USA
3 tablespoons clear honey	3 tablespoons clear honey
3 oz/85g muscovado sugar	½ cup soft dark brown sugar
5 oz/140g soft vegetable margarine	⅓ cup plus 2 tablespoons soft vegetable margarine
2 eggs, beaten	2 eggs, beaten
8 oz/225g self-raising wholemeal flour	2 cups self-rising whole wheat flour
½ teaspoon ground cinnamon	½ teaspoon ground cinnamon
¼ teaspoon ground nutmeg	¼ teaspoon ground nutmeg
1oz/30g desiccated coconut	⅓ cup shredded coconut
4 oz/115g sultanas, or raisins	⅔ cup golden seedless raisins, or raisins
6 oz/170g carrot, scrubbed and finely grated	1 cup carrot, scrubbed and finely shredded
2 tablespoons orange juice	2 tablespoons orange juice
2 tablespoons skimmed milk	2 tablespoons skimmed milk

1. Pre-heat the oven to 325°F/170°C/Gas Mark 3.
2. Grease and flour or line with greaseproof (waxed) paper, a deep, 7-in/18-cm-round cake tin (pan).
3. Put the honey and sugar in a large mixing bowl and cut the margarine into small pieces.
4. Beat together until the mixture is light and fluffy.
5. Beat in the eggs one at a time, mixing in thoroughly.
6. Fold in the remaining ingredients, being careful not to be too heavy handed otherwise you will lose the air you've beaten in and the result will be a heavy-textured cake. The mixture should be quite light and soft.
7. Pour into the prepared tin (pan), smooth the top and bake in the centre of the oven for 50-55 minutes until it is just firm to the touch. It is done when a clean skewer inserted into the cake emerges quite clean.
8. Put the cake on a wire cooling rack and leave for 5 minutes before turning out of the tin (pan).

COCONUT COOKIES

Makes 20

Imperial/Metric	USA
5 oz/140g soft vegetable margarine	½ cup plus 2 tablespoons soft vegetable margarine
2 tablespoons clear honey	2 tablespoons clear honey
3 oz/85g demerara sugar	½ cup raw brown sugar
4 oz/115g rolled oats	1 cup rolled oats
3 oz/85g wholemeal flour	¾ cup whole wheat flour
2 oz/55g desiccated coconut	⅔ cup shredded coconut
2 teaspoons baking powder	2 teaspoons baking powder

1. Pre-heat the oven to 350°F/180°C/Gas Mark 4.

2. Lightly grease 2 baking sheets.

3. Put the margarine, honey and sugar in a large saucepan and heat gently until the margarine has melted, then turn off the heat.

4. In a large bowl, mix together the oats, flour, coconut and baking powder thoroughly, then stir the mixture into the margarine, honey and sugar mixture.

5. Using a teaspoon, put heaped spoonsful on to the baking sheet, spaced well apart.

6. Flatten the cookies lightly with the back of a fork and bake them for 10-15 minutes until they are golden brown, then transfer them straight away to cooling racks to cool, using a palette knife (narrow metal spatula) to lift them. (The cookies crisp up on cooling, so don't expect them to be hard when they come out of the oven and take care not to overcook them as they soon burn.)

7. Once cool, store the cookies in an airtight container.

GINGERBREAD

Cuts into 10 pieces

Imperial/Metric	USA
4 oz/115g fine oatmeal	1 cup fine oatmeal
6 oz/170g wholemeal flour	1½ cups whole wheat flour
1 teaspoon bicarbonate of soda	1 teaspoon baking soda
1½ teaspoons ground ginger	1½ teaspoons ground ginger
½ teaspoon ground cinnamon	½ teaspoon ground cinnamon
4 oz/115g sultanas, or raisins	⅔ cup golden seedless raisins, or raisins
2 tablespoons clear honey	2 tablespoons clear honey
4 tablespoons molasses	4 tablespoons molasses
3 oz/85g soft vegetable margarine	⅓ cup soft vegetable margarine
2 eggs	2 eggs
¼ pt/140ml skimmed milk	⅔ cup skimmed milk

1. Pre-heat the oven to 325°F/170°C/Gas Mark 3.

2. Grease and line a shallow 8-in-20-cm square cake pan.

3. Put the oatmeal in a mixing bowl and sieve (sift) in the flour, bicarbonate of soda (baking soda), ginger and cinnamon and stir in the sultanas (golden seedless raisins), or raisins.

4. Put the honey, molasses and margarine in a saucepan and heat gently until the margarine has melted.

5. Beat the eggs together with the milk.

6. Pour the melted honey, molasses and margarine mixture on to the dry ingredients along with the egg and milk mixture and beat them in quickly until they are thoroughly mixed in.

7. Pour the mixture into the prepared tin (pan) and bake for 50-60 minutes until it is just firm to the touch.

8. Leave to cool in the tin, then turn it out and cut into 10 pieces. Wrap it well and store in an airtight container. Gingerbread will keep for up to a week.

D ATE AND WALNUT LOAF

Makes 1×2 lb/900g loaf

The addition of orange rind and juice gives this family favourite a special flavour and helps to keep it moist, too.

Imperial/Metric	USA
10 oz/285g wholemeal flour	1½ cups whole wheat flour
2 teaspoons baking powder	2 teaspoons baking powder
1 teaspoon ground cinnamon	1 teaspoon ground cinnamon
¼ teaspoon ground nutmeg	¼ teaspoon ground nutmeg
3 oz/85g soft vegetable margarine	⅓ cup soft vegetable margarine
10 oz/285g dates, chopped	1¼ cups dates, chopped
3 oz/85g walnuts, finely chopped	⅔ cup English walnuts, finely chopped
Grated rind of ½ an orange	Shredded rind of ½ an orange
2 oz/55g muscovado sugar	⅓ cup soft dark brown sugar
1 egg	1 egg
¼ pt/140ml skimmed milk	⅔ cup skimmed milk
Juice of 1 orange	Juice of 1 orange

1. Pre-heat the oven to 325°F/170°C/Gas Mark 3.
2. Lightly grease a 2 lb/900g tin (pan) and, if liked, line the bottom with greaseproof (waxed) paper.
3. Put the flour, baking powder, cinnamon and nutmeg in a bowl and rub (cut) in the margarine.
4. Stir in the dates, walnuts, orange rind and sugar.
5. Beat the egg, milk and orange juice together and pour on to the dry ingredients.
6. Mix to a soft consistency and spoon the mixture into the prepared tin (pan).
7. Smooth the top and bake in the centre of the oven for 40 minutes until golden brown. To test whether it's done, insert a skewer into the centre, if it emerges clean, then the loaf is ready. Cool it in the tin on a cooling rack.

COCONUT CRUMBLE

Serves 4-6

Imperial/Metric	USA
4 oz/115g wholemeal flour	1 cup whole wheat flour
1½ oz/45g rolled oats	⅓ cup rolled oats
1½ oz/45g desiccated coconut	½ cup shredded coconut
3 oz/85g soft vegetable margarine	⅓ cup soft vegetable margarine
2 oz/55g demerara sugar	⅓ cup raw brown sugar
½ teaspoon ground cinnamon	½ teaspoon ground cinnamon
1½ lb/680g cooking apples, plums, gooseberries, or rhubarb, prepared	3⅓ cups tart apples, plums, gooseberries, or rhubarb, prepared
Juice of ½ lemon, if using apples	Juice of ½ lemon, if using apples
2 tablespoons cold water	2 tablespoons cold water
1 tablespoon clear honey	1 tablespoon clear honey

1. Pre-heat the oven to 400°F/200°C/Gas Mark 6.

2. Put the flour, oats and coconut in a mixing bowl and stir together.

3. Rub (cut) in the margarine.

4. Stir in the sugar and cinnamon.

5. Put the prepared fruit in the bottom of an ovenproof dish (mixing the apple, if using with the lemon juice to prevent it browning).

6. Spoon over the water and dribble the honey over the fruit, then stir them in.

7. Sprinkle the crumble mixture evenly over the top, smoothing it with a knife.

8. Bake the crumble in the centre of the oven for 25-30 minutes or until the topping is golden and the fruit soft (you may find that you need to reduce the oven temperature for the last 15 minutes to stop the top from becoming too brown, depending on the fruit you use as apples, for example, take longer to cook than rhubarb).

ORGANIC FARM SHOPS

These farm shops are all Soil Association Symbol holders.

ABERDEENSHIRE
West Edingarioch Farm
Premnay
Insch
Aberdeenshire AB5 6PL
0464 20388

Sawmill Croft
Forglen
Turriff
Aberdeenshire AB5 7JY
0888 68501

Craigsglen Organic Farm
West Craigsglen
Craigston
Turriff
Aberdeenshire AB5 7PY
08885 317

3 Cairnleith Croft
Ythanbank
Ellon
Aberdeenshire AB4 0UB
03587 298

Blakeshouse
Crudie
Turriff
Aberdeenshire AB5 7FS
088 85 276

Old Semeil Herb Garden
Strathdon
Aberdeenshire AB3 8XJ
097 52 343

AVON
Leigh Court Farm
Abbotts Leigh
Bristol
Avon BS8 3RA
881 2109

Wraxall House
Wraxall
Nailsea
Avon BS19 1BU
0272 810413

Radford Mill Farm
Timsbury
Bath
Avon BA3 1QF
0761 72549

AYRSHIRE
Auchenkyle
Southwoods Road
Troon
Ayrshire KA10 7EL
0292 311414

8 Back Road
Dailly
Girvan
Ayrshire KA26 9SH
0465 81 247

BEDFORDSHIRE
Rosehaven Organics
110 Cinques Road
Gamlingay
Sandy
Beds SG19 3NR
0767 50142

BERKSHIRE
Ellis Organic Vegetables
64 Blenheim Road
Caversham
Reading
Berks RG4 7RS
0734 473157

BUCKINGHAMSHIRE
Springhill Farm
Dinton
Aylesbury
Bucks HP18 0AD
0296 748278

CAMBRIDGESHIRE
Karma Farm
8 Fen Bank
Isleham
Ely
Cambs CB7 5SL
063 872 1112

Apple Cottage
Button End
Harston
Cambs CB2 5NX
0223 870443

CHANNEL ISLANDS
Organic Produce Ltd
Green Acres Farm
Mont-a-l'Abbe
St Hellier
Jersey
Channel Islands
0534 65303

CLWYD
Fronfawr
Henllan
Denbigh
Clwyd LL16 5DD
074571 2882

CORNWALL
Higher Way Farm
Demelza
St Wenn
Bodmin
Cornwall PL5 5PD
0726 890 489

Penair Gardens
St Clement
Nr Truro
Cornwall TR1 1TD
0872 71937

Haye Farm
Sheviock
Torpoint
Cornwall PL11 3EW
0503 30793

Hewas Field Farm
Trenerth Bridge
Leedstown
Hayle
Cornwall TR27 5ER
0736 850637

Greenlands Organic Produce
Bearah
Bathpool
Launceston
Cornwall PL15 7NW
0579 63060

Stoneybridge Organic Nursery
Tywardreath
Par
Cornwall PL24 2TY
072 681 3858

Tregoose Farm
Newquay
Cornwall TR8 4HU
0637 880344

CUMBRIA
The Village Bakery
Melmerby
Penrith
Cumbria CA10 1HE
0768 81515

DERBYSHIRE
1 Rodsley Lane
Yeaveley
Ashbourne
Derby
Derbyshire DE6 2DT
033 523 594

DEVON
Stallcombe House Farm
Sanctuary Lane
Woodbury Salterton
Exeter
Devon EX5 1EX
0395 32373

Coombe Farm
Cove
Tiverton
Devon EX16 7RU
0398 31808

Lower Turley Farm
Cullompton
Devon EX15 1NG
0884 32234

Hawkerland Home Farm
Sidmouth Road
Aylesbeare
Exeter
Devon EX5 2JJ
0395 32792

11A Thornbury Avenue
Whipton
Exeter
Devon EX1 3HR
0392 64996

The Gardens
Buckland-in-the-Moor
Ashburton
Devon TQ13 7HN
0364 53169

Moorfoot Organic Garden
Denbury
Totnes
Devon TQ9 6DJ
0803 813161

Wyke Hill Gardens
Shobrooke
Crediton
Devon EX17 1AN
0392 851652

Home Park
Rattery
South Brent
Devon TQ10 9LL
03647 3208

East Ackland Farm
Landkey
Barnstaple
Devon EX32 0LD
0271 830216

Marshford Nurseries
Churchill Way
Northam
Bideford
Devon EX39 1NS
023 72 77160

Yalland Farm
South Brent
Devon TQ10 9ED
0364 72287

DORSET
Manor Farm Cottages
Godmanstone
Dorchester
Dorset DT2 7AH
030 03 415

Haygrove Honey Farm
Twyford
Shaftesbury
Dorset SP7 0JF
0747 811855

2 Lower Brimley Coombe Farm
Stoke Abbott
Beaminster
Dorset DT8 3JZ
0308 68419

c/o 15 Victoria Grove
Bridport
Dorset DT6 3AD
0308 24839

Longmeadow
Godmanstone
Dorchester
Dorset DT2 7AE
03003 779

Riverside Farm
Slough Lane
Horton Heath
Nr Wimborne
Dorset BH21 7SL
0202 826509

Bookham Stud
Bishopsdown
Sherborne
Dorset DT9 5PL
096 321 248

Rivermead Farm
Childe Okeford
Blandford
Dorset DT11 8HB
0258 860293

Tamarisk Farm
West Bexington
Dorchester

Dorset DT2 9DF
0308 897784

Lower Berry Court Farm
Donhead St Mary
Nr Shaftesbury
Dorset SP7 9DT
074 788 313

Watcombe Farm
Godmanstone
Dorchester
Dorset DT2 7AD
030 03 295

DUMFRIES
Loch Arthur Village Community
Beeswing
Dumfries DG2 8JQ
038 776 249

DYFED
Little Pencoed
Lawrenny
Kilgetty
Dyfed SA68 0PL
0646 651666

Brynllys
Borth
Dyfed SY24 5LZ
0970 871489

Red House Farm
New Hedges
Tenby
Dyfed SA69 9DP
0834 813 918

Caegu Newtdd Farm
Milo
Llandybie
Ammanford
Dyfed SA18 3LZ
0269 842698

Ty-Hen
Penbryn
Sarnau
Llandysul
Dyfed SA44 6RD
0239 810347

Corgam
Bwlchllan
Lampeter
Dyfed SA48 8QR
097 423 358

Pengelli
Hebron
Whitland
Dyfed SA34 0JX
099 47 481

Derwen Goch
Glandwr
Whitland
Dyfed SA34 0YB
09947 578

Llangloffan Farm
Castle Morris
Haverfordwest
Pembrokeshire
Dyfed SA62 5ET
034 85241

Pencrugiau
Velindre
Crymych
Dyfed SA41 3XH
023986 265

Gellicoedgain
Capel Dewi
Carmarthen
Dyfed SA32 8AF
026 786625

Morvah Nursery
Gwernogle
Carmarthen
Dyfed SA32 7RY
026 789 257

Pentood Uchaf
Cardigan
Dyfed SA43 3NG
0239 612772

Tynrhelyg
Llanrhystud
Dyfed SY23 5EE
097 46 364

Ffynnonwen
Pantybwlch
Newcastle Emlyn
Dyfed SA38 9JF
0559 370276

ESSEX
Anastasis Organic Produce
The Causeway
Highwood Road
Writtle
Essex CM1 3PR
0245 73961

Newhouse Farm
Radwinter
Saffron Walden
Essex CB10 2SP
079987 211

Hicks Farm Partnership
Stockbrook Orchard Farm Shop
Stock Road
Stock
Essex CM4 9PQ
0227 840046

Bluegates Farm
Elmstead Heath
Alresford
Colchester
Essex CO7 8DE
0206 223656

Little Bundish
Threshers Bush
High Laver
Harlow
Essex CM17 0NS
0279 444 663

Boxford Farms Ltd
Hill Farm
Boxford
Colchester
Essex CO6 5NY
0787 210348

Mill Farm
Purleigh
Chelmsford
Essex CM3 8PU
0621 828280

FIFE
Pillars of Hercules
Falkland
Cupar
Fife KY7 7AD
0337 57749

GLAMORGAN
Knelston Hall Farm
Knelston
Reynoldston
Swansea
Glamorgan SA3 1AR
0792 390062

Pencoed Organic Growers
Felindre Nurseries
Felindre

Pencoed
Bridgend
Glamorgan CF35 5HU
0656 861956

Llwyn Ifan Ddu Farm
Garnswllt Road
Pontardulais
Glamorgan SA4 1QJ
0269 2090

GLOUCESTER
Hatherop Market Garden
76A Church Road
Quenington
Cirencester
Glos GL7 5BL
028575 326/493

GWYNEDD
Tyddyn Berth
Rhosfawr
Y-Ffor
Pwllheli
Gwynedd LL53 6YA
076 688 545

HAMPSHIRE
'The Anchorage'
Salisbury Road
Broughton
Nr Stockbridge
Hants SO20 8DX
0794 301 234

Larks Barrow Market Garden
Kingsclere Road
Whitchurch
Hants RG28 7QB
025 682 892253

Cumbers Farm
Rogate
Petersfield
Hants GU31 5DB
073 080 840

HEREFORDSHIRE

Upper Bache Farm
Kimbolton
Leominster
Herefds HR6 0EP
0568 4409

Prospect Cottage
Bartestree
Hereford
Herefds HR1 4BY
0432 851164

Priors Grove
Putley
Ledbury
Herefds HR8 2RE
053 183 511

Lilly Hall Farm
Ledbury
Herefds HR8 2LD
0531 2892

Green Acres
Dinmore
Hereford
Herefds HR4 8ED
056 884 7045

Vicarage Cottage
Canon Frome
Ledbury
Herefds HR8 2TD
053 183 534

Batchley
Bredenbury
Bromyard
Herefds HR7 4TH
0885 483377

Canon Frome Court
Canon Frome
Ledbury

Herefds HR8 2TD
053 183 497

Elm Grove
Thornbury
Bromyard
Herefds HR7 4NJ
0885 410204

Oak Cottage
The Riddox
Nr Pembridge
Hereford
Herefds HR6 9JS
0544 318479

HUMBERSIDE

Arvensis
Ferry Road
Barrow on Humber
Humberside DN19 7HB
0469 31188

KENT

Perry Court Farm
Petham
Canterbury
Kent CT4 5RU
0227 738 449

Mr P J Zeen
Pollards Dane
Canterbury Road
Charing
Ashford
Kent TN27 0EX
023 371 2580

Luddlesdown Organic Farms Ltd
Luddlesdown
Nr Cobham
Kent DA13 0XE
0474 813376

Drudgeon Farm
Bean
Nr Dartford
Kent DA2 8AP
047 483 3186

Briar Rose
Pett Lane
Stockbury
Sittingbourne
Kent ME9 7RL
062 784318

Woolton Farm
Bekesbourne
Canterbury
Kent CT4 5EA
0227 830525

LANCASHIRE
Bank House Farm
Silverdale
Carnforth
Lancs LA5 0RE
0524 701280

Ferrocrete Farm
Arkholme
Carnforth
Lancs LA6 1AU
0468 21965

LEICESTERSHIRE
Cheval House
South Kilworth
Lutterworth
Leics L17 6DX
0858 575309

LINCOLNSHIRE
Hermitage Farm
Havenbank Road
New York
Lincs LN4 4XJ
020573 286

Hyland Farm
Croft
Skegness
Lincs PE24 4RZ
0754 2921

Eden Nurseries
Rectory Lane
Old Bolingbroke
Spilsby
Lincs PE23 4EY
07903 582

South View
Trader Bank
Sibsey
Boston
Lincs PE22 0UJ
0205 750470

NORFOLK
Mangreen Garden
Mangreen
Swardeston
Norwich
Norfolk NR14 8DD
0508 70444

Ms M Wilson
Ferry Farm
Oxborough
Kings Lynn
Norfolk PE33 9PT
036 621 287

Mangreen Hall Farm
Swardeston
Norwich
Norfolk NR14 8DD
0508 78710

Loke Cottage
4 Scarning Fen
East Dereham
Norfolk NR19 1LN
0362 695947

Anchor Farm
Wood Lane
Little Ellingham
Norfolk NR17 1JZ
0953 453057

Bridge Farm
Norwich Road
New Costessey
Norwich
Norfolk NR5 0LA
0603 742822

1 Bizewell Cottages
Coast Road
Trimingham
Norwich
Norfolk NR11 8HY
026 378 675

Village Farm
Market Weston
Diss
Norfolk IP22 2NZ
035921 240

NORTHUMBERLAND
Brackenside
Bausden
Berwick on Tweed
Northumberland TD15 2TQ
0289 88293

NOTTINGHAMSHIRE
Boundary House
Girton
Newark
Notts NG23 7MX
052277 760

Bumblebee Hall
Westbrook Lane
South Collingham
Newark
Notts NG23 7RE
0636 892638

R & S Contracts Ltd
21 Kighill Lane
Ravenshead
Nottingham
Notts NG15 9HN
0623 794648

OXFORDSHIRE
Path Hill Farm Cottage
Whitchurch
Nr Reading
Oxon RG8 7RE
07357 2365

1 Field Farm Cottages
Faringdon Road
Longcot
Oxon SN7 7UA
0793 783421

PERTHSHIRE
Drummawhance Farm
Auchterarder
Perthshire PH3 1NP
076 481 267

South West Fullerton
Miegle
Perthshire PH12 8SN
082 84 391

POWYS
Riandi
Erwood
Builth Wells
Powys LD2 3AJ
098 23 230

Neuadd Fach
Talgarth
Brecon
Powys LD3 0HA
0874 711307

Primrose Farm
Felindre
Brecon
Powys LD3 0ST
049 74636

Caebalciog Farm
St Harmon
Rhayader
Powys LD6 5LU

SHROPSHIRE
Lea Hall
Harmer Hill
Shrewsbury
Shropshire SY4 3DY
0939 290 342

The Poplars
Bwern-y-Brenin
Oswestry
Shropshire SY10 8AR
0691 652166

Plealey Villa
Pontesbury
Shrewsbury
Shropshire SY5 0XT
0743 860304

SOMERSET
Maidencroft Farm
Higher Wick
Glastonbury
Somerset BA6 8JN
0458 32752

Oake Bridge Farm
Oake
Taunton
Somerset TA4 1AY
0823 461317

2 Manor Cottages
Shepton Montague

Wincanton
Somerset BA9 8JB
0749 812571

Avalon Vineyard
The Drive
East Pennard
Shepton Mallet
Somerset TA3 6UA
074 986 393

STAFFORDSHIRE
Grange Farm
Hollies Lane
Pattingham
Wolverhampton
Staffs WV6 7HJ
0902 700248

Crowtree Farm
Loxley
Uttoxeter
Staffs ST14 8RX
0889 565806

Staffs College of Agriculture
Rodbaston
Penkridge
Staffs ST19 5PH
078571 2209

SUFFOLK
Bushy Ley Cottage
Offton Road
Elmsett
Ipswich
Suffolk IP7 6PQ
047 333 671

Trickers Farm
Kersey
Ipswich
Suffolk IP7 6EW
0473 827231

SURREY

Barn Field Organic Produce
Franksfield
Peaslake
Guildford
Surrey GU5 9SR
0306 731310

SUSSEX

Laines Organic Farm
47 Newberry Lane
Cuckfield
West Sussex
Sussex RH17 5AA
0444 452 633

The Jacketings Organic Nursery
Underhill Lane
Clayton
Sussex BN6 9PL
079 18 2323

Barklye Farm
Swife Lane
Broad Oak
Heathfield
Sussex TN21 8UR
0435 883536

Bramley Farm
Bodiam
Robertsbridge
East Sussex
TN32 5RJ
058 083 566

Sky Farm
Swife Lane
Broad Oak
Heathfield
Sussex TN21 8UR
0435 882167

3 Whitestone Farm
Birdham

Chichester
Sussex PO20 7HU
0243 512416

Old Plaw Hatch
Sharpthorne
East Grinstead
West Sussex
RH19 4JL
0342 810857

Busses Farm
Harwoods Lane
East Grinstead
West Sussex
RH19 4NL
0342 321749

Malthouse Cottage Farm
Malthouse Lane
Ashington
Pulborough
Sussex RH20 3BU
0903 892456

Boat House Farm
Isfield
Sussex TN22 5TY
0825 302

Scragoak Farm
Brightling Road
Robertsbridge
East Sussex
TN32 5HB
042 482 364

Sedlescombe Vineyards
Robertsbridge
East Sussex
TN32 5SA
058 083 715

WARWICKSHIRE
Bramcote Mains
Wolvey Road
Bulkington
Nuneaton
Warwks CV12 9JX
0455 220441

WILTSHIRE
Furze Cottage
Teffont Magna
Nr Salisbury
Wilts SP3 5QU
072276 285

Whitbourne Farm
Corsley
Warminster
Wilts BA12 7QJ
037 388 205

WORCESTERSHIRE
Blackberry Farm
Russell Street
Great Comberton
Pershore
Worcs WR10 3DT
0386 74275

Temple Oak House
Broughton Green
Hanbury
Droitwich
Worcs WR9 7EF
090 569 683

Temple Laugherne House
Lower Broadheath
Worcs WR2 6RS
0905 641122

YORKSHIRE
Church House

Shackleton
Hovingham
Yorks YO6 4NB
065 382 474

Brickyard Farm
Badsworth
Nr Pontefract
Yorks WF9 1AX
0977 617327

Eddlethorpe Hall
Malton
North Yorks
Yorks YO17 9QS
065 385 218

Bracken Farm
Priestley Green
Norwood Green
Halifax
Yorks HX3 8RQ
0422 205578

Standfield Hall Farm
Westgate Carr Road
Pickering
North Yorks YO18 8LX
0751 72249

Kyle Cottage
Tollerton
North Yorks YO6 2EQ
03473 8169

Meanwood Valley Urban Farm
Sugarwell Road
Meanwood
Leeds
Yorks LS7 2QG
0532 629759

USEFUL ADDRESSES

Centre for Alternative Technology
Llywyngwern Quarry, Machynlleth, Powys

Energy Efficiency Office
Department of Energy, Thames House South, Millbank, London SW19 4QJ

Friends of the Earth
26-28 Underwood Street, London N1 7JU

Greenpeace
30-31 Islington Green, London N1 8XE

The Henry Doubleday Research Association
Ryton-on-Dunsmore, Coventry CV8 3LG

***Here's Health* Magazine**
Victory House, Leicester Place, London WC2H 7QP

The Soil Association
86-88 Colston Street, Bristol BS1 5BB

Vegetarian Society
Parkdale, Dunham Road, Altrincham, Chesire WA14 4QG

AUSTRALIA
Friends of the Earth
56 Foster Street, Surry Hills 2010, NSW and
222 Brunswick Street, Fitzroy 3065, Victoria

Greenpeace
37 Nicholson Street, Balmain 2041, NSW

Australian Conservation Association
NSW: 18 Argyle Street, Sydney 2000
VIC: 240 Gore Street, Fitzroy 3065

FURTHER READING

Button, John, *How to be Green*, (Century, 1989)
Button, John, *Green Pages*, (Macdonald Optima, 1988)
Davies, Dr Stephen and Stewart, Dr Alan, *Nutritional Medicine*, (Pan, 1987)
Elkington, John and Hailes, Julia, *Green Consumer Guide*, (Gollancz, 1988)
Icke, David, *It Doesn't Have to be Like This*, (Green Print, 1990)
Mabey, David and Gear, Alan and Jackie, *Thorsons Organic Consumer Guide*, (Thorsons, 1990)

SUBJECT INDEX

RECIPE INDEX